# WINSLOW HOMER

and the

# POETICS OF PLACE

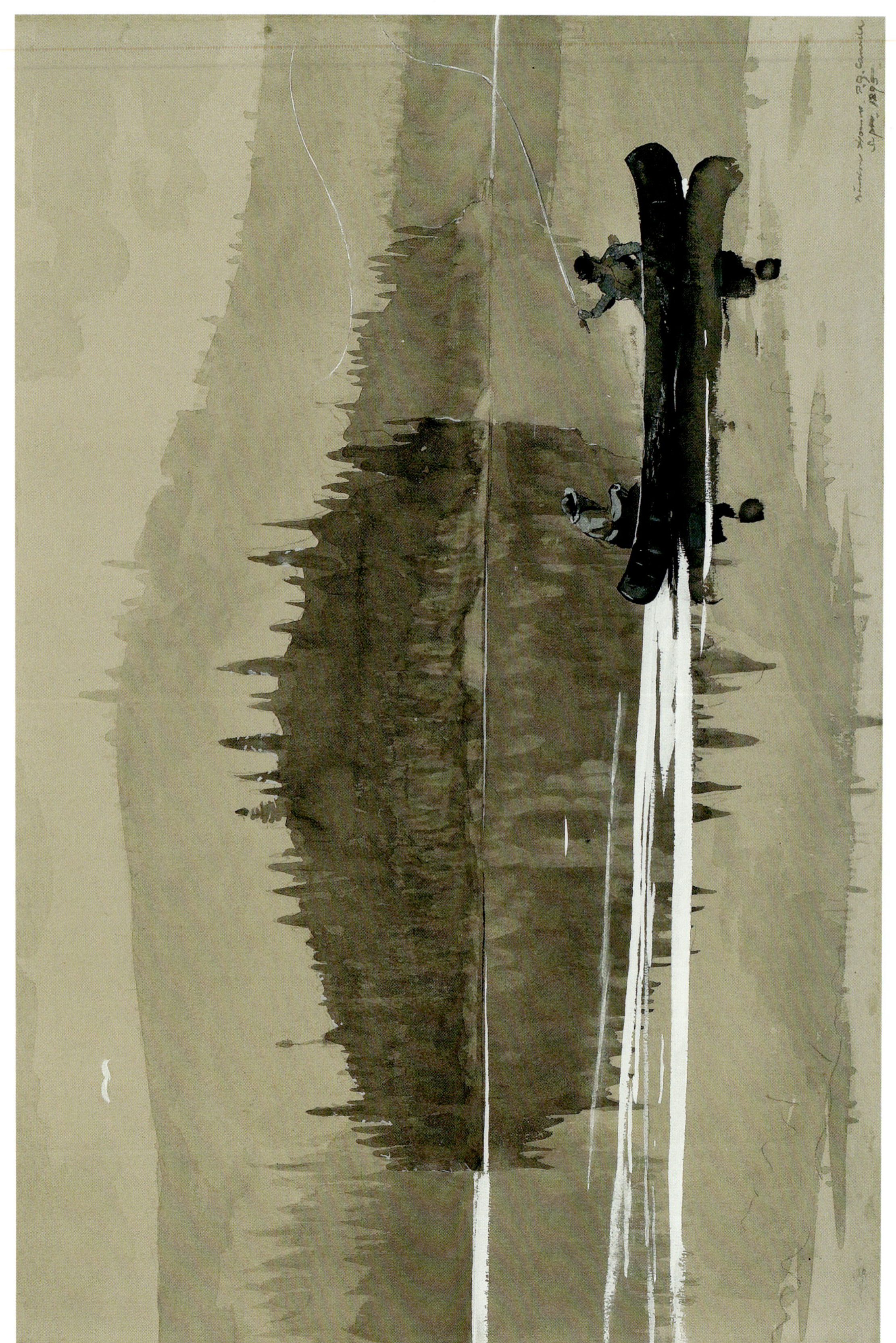

# WINSLOW HOMER
## AND THE
# POETICS OF PLACE

Thomas Andrew Denenberg

PORTLAND MUSEUM OF ART
PORTLAND, MAINE

## DIRECTOR'S FOREWORD

This book marks the centennial of the death of Winslow Homer (1836–1910). One hundred years after the great painter passed from the American scene, the role of the United States in the world is shifting, leading to a national search for the qualities that define the country. A new "Americanness" is in the air and under close consideration. What are our values and how do we identify ourselves when our culture grows ever more global? Ironically, these questions often lead us to turn inward toward region and, ultimately, to the issue of place. What role, we may ask, did Maine play in the construction of a national identity? Maine—beloved for the same reasons that brought Homer here more than a century ago—possesses an aura of authenticity and a full measure of potential and risk. Today, as in the late nineteenth century, Maine provides an answer for people experiencing an alienation from nature and desiring a different texture to everyday life.

Winslow Homer is an archetype of those who visited the state of Maine and chose to put down roots. He remains one of our most beloved American artists, as popular in Europe as on native shores. Of the moment, bridging the past, and a harbinger of the future, Homer's work has—like that of no other artist in America—grasped an age by presenting the culmination of one era and the potential of the next. His defining moment arrived when he moved to Scarborough in 1883. There, at Prouts Neck, he produced a body of work representing a young nation preparing to manifest a new identity and destiny. Homer's fame is persistent because it is inextricably linked to the globalization of American culture and the rise of what is now known as the American Century.

Homer's relationship to the Portland Museum of Art is long-standing and intimate. He first exhibited with the institution—then known as the Portland Society of Art—in 1893, and his legacy runs throughout our galleries in his art, as well as in that of those who followed. The Charles Shipman Payson Building, constructed in 1983, completed the transformation of the Portland Society of Art into the Portland Museum of Art, and the Payson Collection established the Museum as a major repository of Homer's work. Since that time, Peggy and Harold Osher have generously donated a comprehensive collection of Homer's graphic work, Barbro and Bernard Osher bestowed the magnificent painting *Sharpshooter*, the family of Lily Russell bequeathed *Girl Seated on Hillside Overlooking the Water*, and William Hamill has given an important graphite portrait to the Museum. Nearly twenty-five years after the opening of the Payson Building, the Museum intensified its growing Homer legacy by acquiring the Winslow Homer Studio, making Maine and the Portland Museum of Art a center for this important painter. Through his art and influence, Homer is the lynchpin to our great collecting traditions.

As we mark this passage of time by presenting our collection to the community, we would like once again to thank those who have entrusted their works by Winslow Homer to the Portland Museum of Art. Your generosity has made the Museum a living home for the painter that will inspire the next generation of great artists who live and work in Maine.

**MARK H. C. BESSIRE**
**DIRECTOR**

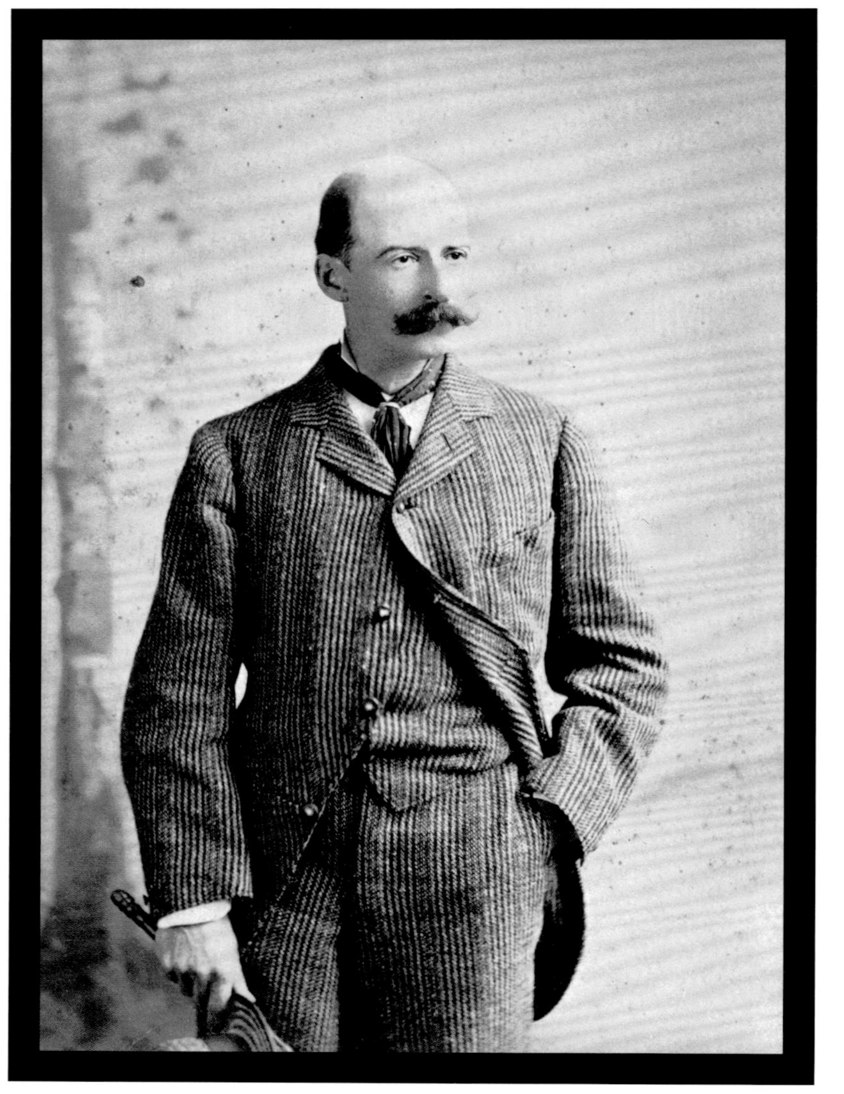

FIG. 1

# WINSLOW HOMER AND THE POETICS OF PLACE

Thomas Andrew Denenberg

A poetics of place runs through the work of Winslow Homer. Based on lived experience and a penchant for close observation, this regard for the local and the immediate unifies Homer's half century of creative life. Homer's poetics trade in inflection and implication. They trace his interest in authenticity yet reveal an eye for irony—even jocularity. Homer's poetics are literal, metaphoric, nostalgic, and frank. They are built upon the telling detail that becomes a mnemonic, the flick of the brush that conjures a memory, builds a narrative yet leaves the final chapter unwritten, the moral untold. Above all, Homer's visual language seeks to ground the viewer in a landscape of the mind during an era that challenged traditional notions of terra firma in America.

Homer lived in extraordinary times and enjoyed remarkable experiences. Born in 1836 and dying in 1910, he was of an age to converse with men who fired on British regulars as well as with those who commuted to Wall Street. As a young man, he followed the march and bore witness to a bloodletting of epic proportions during the sectional crises of the American Civil War. As Homer approached maturity, the pace of modernity brought fundamental change to daily life in the United States and profoundly complicated perceptions of place. Towns grew quaint as cities came to dominate American culture. Corporations organized commerce across state lines. Rapid improvements in travel and communication, coupled with unparalleled social and geographic mobility, lent a new sense of velocity to the voyage of life.

Homer, from a family of businessmen, internalized the complexities and ambivalences of his age. As the popular image of the artist coalesced around bohemian stereotypes in the later half of the nineteenth century, Homer instead cultivated a Janus-faced public persona, styling himself by turns as a captain of industry and the "hermit of Prouts Neck" after his family purchased land in that summer colony in 1883 (fig. 1). Well-traveled, well-read, and well-dressed, Homer enjoyed the comforts made available by industrial capitalism yet simultaneously eschewed the trappings of bourgeois life in search of authentic experience in a world increasingly untethered from the ties of traditional social economy.

## SIGHT AND SITE

Homer's oeuvre is multivalent. He is one of a handful of American artists to achieve a reputation in multiple media, initially working as an apprentice lithographer, then turning to commercial illustration, painting, watercolor, and printmaking. His work is at once accessible and elliptical. Running against the tide of popular opinion, the notion that "a picture which does not tell its own story is but half a picture," Homer was ever-willing to leave a narrative silence in his art, both graphic and fine.[1] Homer's image of a sharpshooter—which appeared in two formats, an engraving and a painting—is an early example of his ability to tell a story without an ending. The image, debuting in the popular imagination as a wood engraving (fig. 2) reproduced in *Harper's Weekly* in November of 1862, bore the legend "*The Army of the Potomac—A Sharp-Shooter on Picket Duty*. (From a Painting by W. Homer, Esq.)." The parenthetical caption has puzzled students for generations because Homer did not sign the work until 1863 or exhibit it publicly for some months thereafter. However, whether the paint was dry when the woodcut was published matters less than the subtle differences between the two versions and the cultural work of each image.

For the 120,000 subscribers who paid $2.50 a year for the five-year-old magazine, Homer's *Sharp-Shooter* arrived by mail and signaled a shift in the visual reportage of the American Civil War.[2] The conflict, which had begun in April of the previous year with a formal barrage upon Fort Sumter followed by the jejune clash of volunteers at Bull Run, had by the autumn of 1862 become a sobering and sanguinary affair.

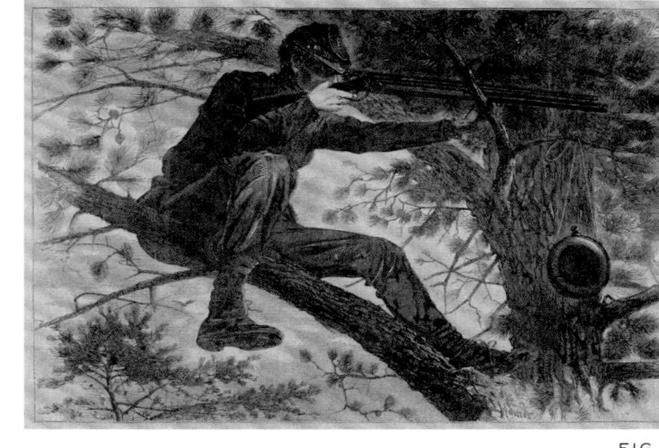

FIG. 2

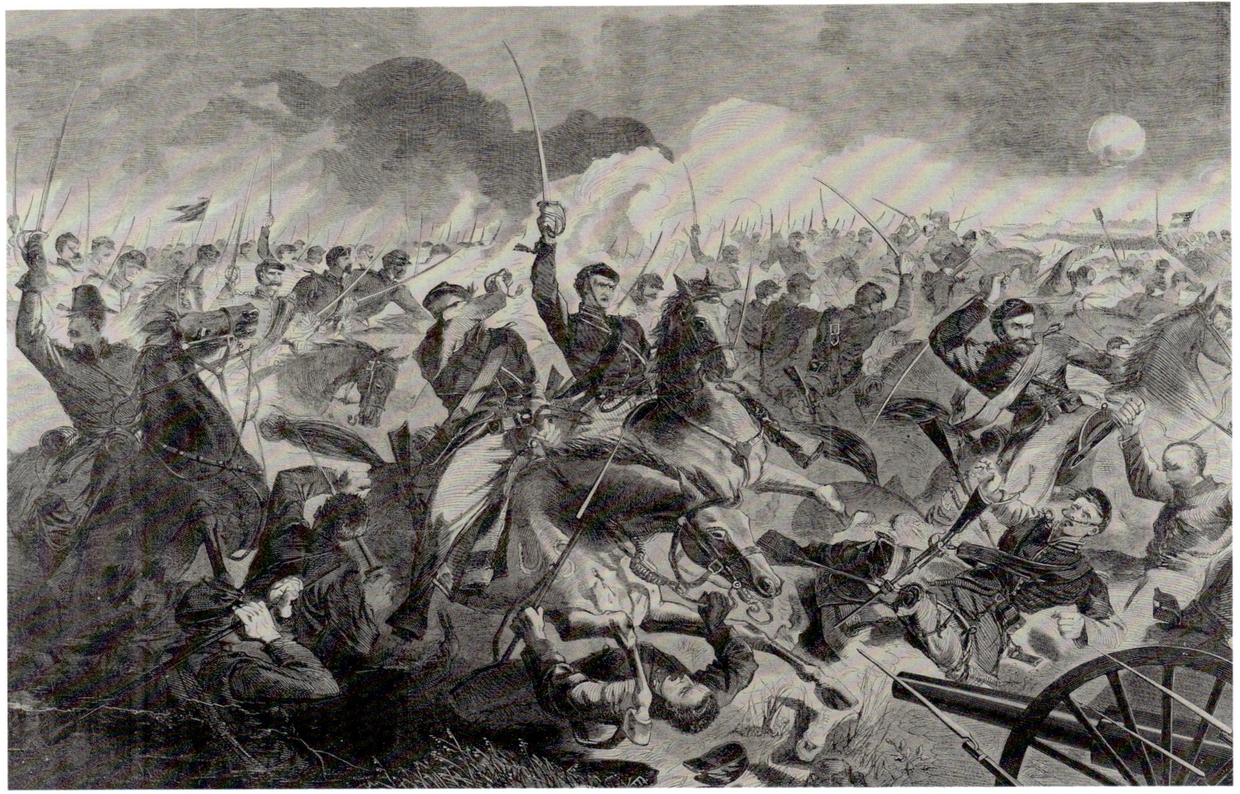

FIG. 3

Seven sharp clashes during the Peninsula Campaign, a second large battle at Manassas, and the fierce carnage of Antietam in September—the single bloodiest day in American history—riveted the attention of a population that held a lingering belief in the nobility of arms. The songs and banners of 1861 that had accompanied Abraham Lincoln's call for ninety-day troops to suppress the rebellion receded in popular memory, and both sides moved to develop the military infrastructure required to pursue hostilities at length and to the bitter end. The war matured in 1862, and this, then, is the moment captured by Homer.

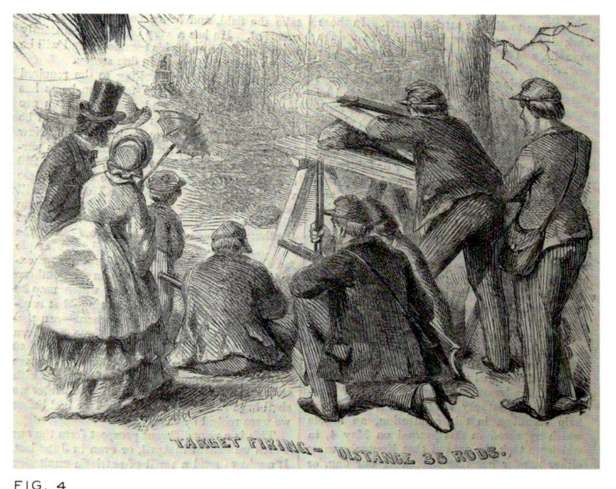


FIG. 4

Gone, by the time of *A Sharp-Shooter*, were romantic images of flags unfurled, flashing sabers, and batteries overrun by natty cavalrymen (fig. 3). Past was the lighthearted notion that using a bench-rest rifle in combat was little more than target shooting—a supposition implied by *Harper's* the previous autumn, when the magazine featured a montage on the cover to illustrate a brief article on Berdan's Sharpshooters, one of the Union's most celebrated regiments. In these early days of the war, this cover depicted a carnival-like atmosphere in camp, with vignettes of soldiers loading and firing target rifles under the approving eyes of men in top hats and women in crinolines (fig. 4). In the accompanying article, little mention is made of the cover imagery, but great emphasis is placed on the morality of the men from New Hampshire in the regiment, relying on a popular stereotype of the steady habits found in northern New England. This focus on character is revealing, for popular opinion on the role of the sharpshooter in battle was evolving and mixed. *Harper's* reassured the reading public that the "right sort" of men were employed in the new, morally challenging practice.

The act of intimate killing returned to the battlefield during the Civil War with the utilization of elite soldiers designated as sharpshooters. Prior to the conflict, infantry tactics prized maneuvering to effect surrender, retreat, or the terrible, but anonymous, punishment meted out by large formations of soldiers armed with single-shot, smoothbore long arms firing in volleys. In earlier European conflicts, political realities conspired to prohibit targeting individuals—especially officers—even when the advent of the rifle allowed for such opportunity. Sectional hostilities in America, however, quickly peeled back this veneer of gallantry and redirected established rules of war. Deliberately targeting an opponent became acceptable, even desirable.

"Civil War killing," writes historian Drew Gilpin Faust, "required work—intellectual and psychological effort to address religious and emotional constraints, as well as adaptations to the ways this particular war's technologies, tactics, and logistics shaped the experience of combat."[3] Homer himself commented on this effort in old age, when he recalled in a letter, "I looked through one of their rifles once . . . the above impression struck me as being as near murder as anything I ever could think of in connection with the army & I always had a horror of that branch of the service."[4] The painter added emphasis in the margins with a small drawing of a man caught in the crosshairs of a telescopic sight (fig. 5). The ability to optically enhance the distant combatant and draw him near is the crux of *A Sharp-Shooter*.

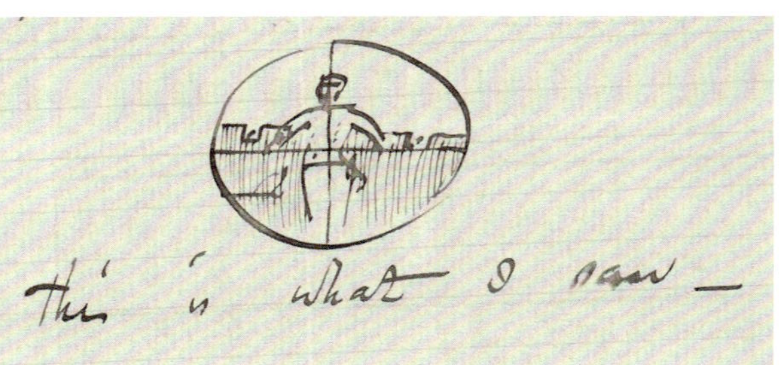


FIG. 5

The advent of the telescopic sight collapsed distance—literal and moral—and added to the destabilization of place in the modern psyche. Period literature commented on the unseemly phenomenon of a "forced" bullet from a rifle traveling faster than the speed of sound. The soldier, for the first time, never knew what hit him.

The American sectional conflict is often cited as the first modern war. "Mid-nineteenth century armies," writes military historian John Keegan, "hovered on the brink of true modernization, half belonging to the military past, when martial vigor and number were alone thought to count, but already entering the military future, when technology would predominate."[5] Beyond telescopic sights, the list of emerging technologies employed and perfected during the conflict is long and sobering. Repeating rifles, ironclad ships, railroads, the telegraph, aerial observation from bal-

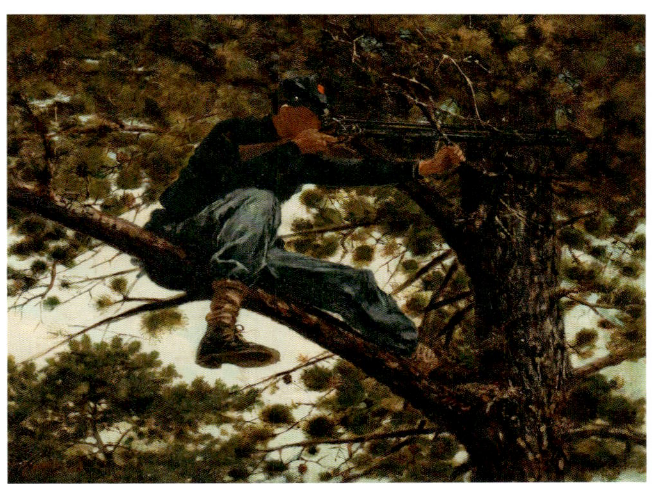

FIG. 6

loons, and indirect artillery fire—to say nothing of machine-stitched shoes, standard sizes for uniforms, and a host of mundane, but critical, logistical contributions to the cause—all owe their origins to the war. Lost in this accounting, however, is the human denominator—an emotional tally for the experience of modern combat. *A Sharp-Shooter*'s second incarnation, as an oil painting, is one such reckoning, for Homer revisited the image of the man in a tree and reemphasized the dangers of place.

*Sharpshooter* (fig. 6), identified by Homer's first biographer, William Howe Downes, as the artist's debut work in oil, is on one level a pragmatic painting.[6] Diminutive and closely cropped, it trades in authenticity rather than in scale to claim authority. Homer's eye for detail, schooled by his career as an illustrator, is on full display. As in the earlier wood engraving, the soldier is wearing the easily recognizable fatigue uniform of the Union army—sack coat, trousers, brogans, and a forage cap. Homer even depicts the common practice of blousing trousers into wool socks, rather than wearing leggings provided by the quartermaster. Furthermore, the artist exploits his new oil medium to render the soldier's wool trousers in regulation sky blue and to feature a then-recent addition to the uniform, a small patch of red fabric on the crown of the soldier's cap designating the protagonist as belonging to the First Division of the Third Corps of the Army of the Potomac. The weapon itself is typical of the specialized civilian long arms produced by gunsmiths such as Abe Williams, Morgan James, and George Ferris which found favor with sharpshooters in the Northern army. Such verisimilitude served notice that *Sharpshooter* was a new model of martial painting, born of intimate knowledge.

Homer's time at the front provided experiences that shaped his worldview. Initially in Virginia for the fall campaign of 1861 at the behest of *Harper's*, Homer returned there in the spring of 1862. His mother, writing that summer, noticed a change in her son after the trip. "Winslow," she wrote, "went to the war front of Yorktown & camped out about two months. He suffered much, was without food 3 days at a time & all in camp either died or were carried away with typhoid fever . . . He came home so changed that his best friends did not know him."[7] The deprivations Homer endured and the violence he witnessed lend his subsequent paintings a cool authority rarely seen on canvas.

*Sharpshooter*—minutely accurate—derives its chilling nature from a simple gesture. Homer chose to depict his soldier without a face. The artist, though profoundly interested in detail, decided to essentialize his sharpshooter—to render the specialist universal. The soldier, so carefully delineated and consciously located, becomes death itself—cold and calculating. Furthermore, Homer froze the moment in time. There is a finger on the trigger, but no puff of smoke to relieve the tension. This became a favorite strategy of Homer's, notes art historian Franklin Kelly. Writing of *The Gulf Stream*—a work from some thirty years later—Kelly marvels at the painter's ability to suspend "the story at an almost unbearably tense moment . . . leaving the question of this particular man's fate unanswered." In doing so, "Homer deflected the narrative . . . away from the specific."[8] *Sharpshooter*, like *The Gulf Stream* and so many paintings now understood as national treasures, evidences Homer's ability to fix the largest concerns of modern men and women on the canvas. Homer's soldier, eyeing his victim—yet cropped as if caught in a telescopic sight himself—is trapped in the terrible logic of war.

## A COUNTRY SKETCH

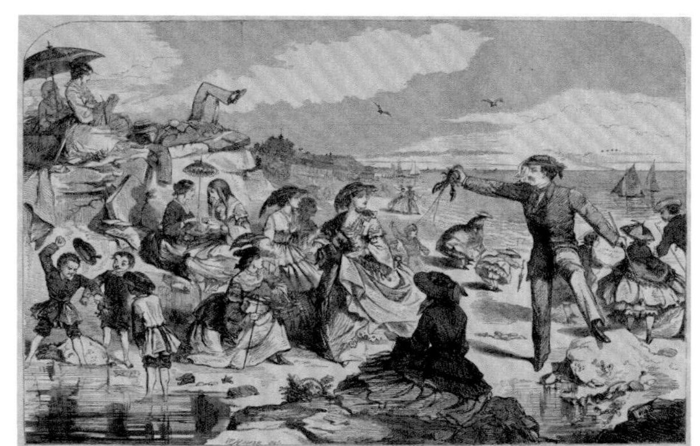

FIG. 7

Winslow Homer possessed an ironic, even an arch, temperament. He illustrated his letters with caricatures, frequently engaging in self-deprecating visual banter. Although Homer was particularly well equipped to paint the darkest of subject matter—witness *Sharpshooter*—he displayed a rich sense of humor in his graphic work. Playing to the crowd as an illustrator has a long and distinguished tradition, and Homer's often marginal and subtextual vignettes testify to his recognition and command of the conventions of the medium. An errant bottle rocket on the Fourth of July or a dandy shaking a lobster at a pretty girl is to be expected of the rollicking nature of popular visual culture in the last half of the nineteenth century (fig. 7). It is in the traditionally sober medium of oil painting, however, that Homer's humor emerges most fully. It is in this genre that Homer reveals his subversive nature and proves to be a master of what art historian Jennifer Greenhill has called "visual deadpan."[9] The ability to quietly—even covertly—lampoon in paint is an art unto itself. Nowhere is the puckish Homer more on view than in *Artists Sketching in the White Mountains* (fig. 8), from 1868.

At first glance, *Artists Sketching* comes across without guile. Identified by art historian Robert McGrath as depicting a spot in the Intervale above North Conway, New Hampshire, Homer's diminutive painting purports to capture what White Mountain booster the Reverend Thomas Starr King called "a large nocturnal poem in the landscape."[10] Long the subject of creative attention, the Intervale offered sweeping views of the Presidential Range from a unique, low-lying vantage point that heightened the drama of the scene, yet provided a majestic panorama. As early as 1855,

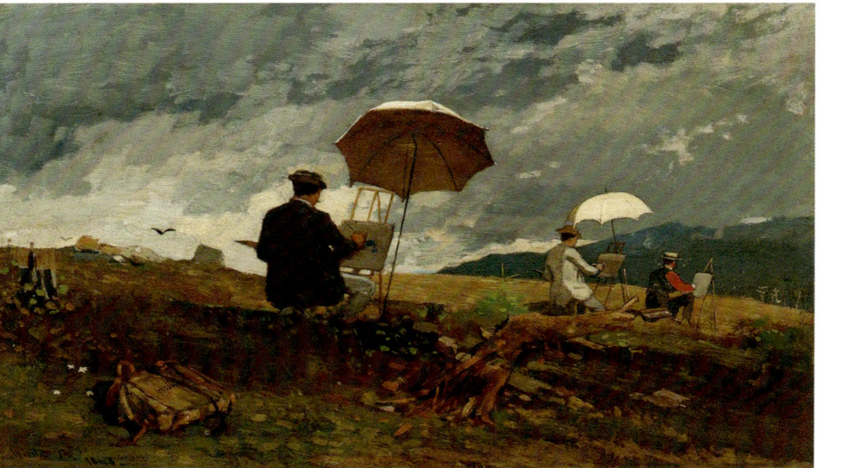

FIG. 8

a popular journal for artists noted that the area around North Conway had become "the pet valley of our landscape painters. There are always a dozen or more here during the sketching season, and you can hardly glance over the meadows in any direction, without seeing one of their white umbrellas shining in the sun."[11] By the 1860s, to be taken seriously as an artist required at least one pilgrimage to paint Mount Washington. Indeed, Thomas Cole, Asher Durand, Benjamin Champney, Alfred Thompson Bricher, Jasper Cropsey, Thomas Doughty, John Kensett, and Albert Bierstadt all made views of the White Mountains their stock in trade.

*Artists Sketching*, however, was born of reasons more mercenary than creative, as Homer traveled to the White Mountains on assignment from *Harper's Weekly* and *Appletons' Journal* in the spring of 1869. His assignment: capture the culture of summer. "What should we do without our vacations?" asked *Appletons'* in an article from that summer. "How could we endure the monotony of professional labors, or of city occupations, if the summer months every-year did not seduce us into the fields and mountains?"[12]

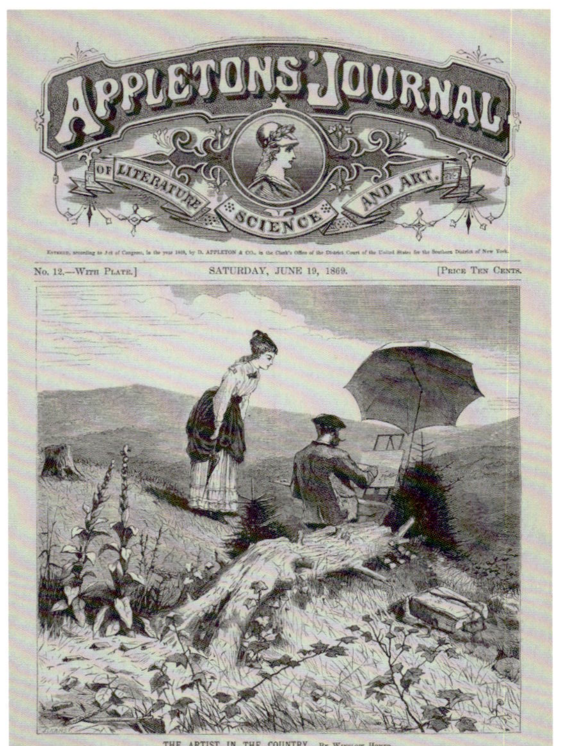


FIG. 9

Illustrations born of the trip appeared in both magazines, and in June of 1869, the cover of *Appletons'* featured a variation on *Artists Sketching* as a wood engraving (fig. 9). The image is a closely cropped view of a painter leaning intently over his easel, the figure rendered supercilious by a woman standing over him, literally looking over his shoulder. Should *Appletons'* readers miss the humor in the scene, the accompanying article makes grand sport of tensions cropping up in the era as the new middle class took to the mountains for their summer holiday. Playing off the novelty of ladies of leisure in such a rural setting, *Appletons'* proposes a spoof on gender relations: "As to the painter's companion in Mr. Winslow Homer's sketch, we will let our readers form what romance pertaining to her they may please. A love-story could be woven out of the situation, although some crusty critic might declare that the man is far too much absorbed in his labors, too utterly heedless of the young woman at his elbow, for their relationship to be any thing else but that of man and wife."[13] The overt humor of the cover is reinforced by the benign misogyny of the article. As cultural historian Roger Stein has noted, Homer's graphic work shifted from "vague poetic appeal" in this period to a "tightly organized drama of contrasts" that made for humorous comment on the gender politics of the age.[14] The painting that Homer worked up from his trip to the White Mountains proved to be equally humorous, although the punch line is softer.

*Artists Sketching* is a small canvas but a large, self-deprecating poke at Homer, his employers, his colleagues, and the state of American painting. Although the artists in the scene are frequently identified as Homer Dodge Martin, John Fitch, and Homer himself, the painter leaves only the latter without ambiguity by signing his name on the knapsack. Filling the picture frame with his three central characters, Homer once again leaves off the subject of their attention. As in *Sharpshooter*, Homer deflects the narrative and sets up a visual pun by placing himself at the end of a line of painters queued up to paint the glories of the White Mountains: three swells in the country, protected from the sun by umbrellas. Should Homer's viewer have any doubt as to his delight in the irony of being the caboose in the composition, Homer reworked the stump at left, lowering its visual impact but raising the comedic ante by including a bottle of wine.

Homer's send-up of the culture of summer in New England in 1868 presaged the development of the region as a tourist landscape. His humorous turn at the parade of painters converting scenery into a commodity documents an age-old Gordian knot for artists; the taste for landscape painting is predicated upon taking in the view. Tourists make demands upon the environment, however, that quickly undermine the promise of authentic experience. Trains to the White Mountains, hotels in their valleys, and carriages to the summit of Mount Washington all conspire to erode the scene, literally and metaphorically. As one watering hole becomes too popular, those in the know move on to places where the promise of a rugged view is extended. Homer, based in Boston and then New York, but habitually peripatetic, found such a place at Prouts Neck, a spit of land jutting out into the Atlantic Ocean in Scarborough, Maine. At Prouts Neck, Homer self-consciously retreated from society—loudly performing the role of hermit/artist—and executed a series of paintings depicting the many moods of the sea.

## CLEFT FOR ME

*Weatherbeaten* is a paradigm (fig. 10). It is a way of understanding the sea change in popular perception of the New England coast under way in the decades that bracketed the turn of the century. Prior to Homer's final confrontation with the timeless drama playing out on the rocks before his studio at Prouts Neck, the region had been, to use art historian Sarah Burns's phrase, "painted out."[15] The penchant for artists and writers to frame New England as a nostalgic landscape marked by aged gentility—burnished at best, more often hoary—engendered a popular notion that the region was well past its prime. Autumnal landscapes, weathered buildings, even the quiescence of the waves in seascapes of the 1870s, suggested a calm, halcyon perception of place in the decade after the Civil War. In contrast, Homer's Prouts Neck paintings of the 1890s—the apogee of a career dedicated to firsthand experience, observation, and the mastery of visual narrative—injected vitality, even virility, back into the New England scene.

*Weatherbeaten*, a landscape without figures, is a powerful work and was received as such. Frederick Morton, a leading critic, wrote in 1902 that "all of Homer's experience and practice in figure painting and landscape have led up to his inimitable seascapes, which he paints as no other artist ever did or can."[16] The authority of the work—the coast limned as no other "ever did or can"—is captured by Downes, who wrote in 1911 that one "cannot stand before a picture like *Storm-Beaten* without being mentally stimulated and exalted; such is the potency of a personal imagination working with natural fact for its sole material . . . reality is made more real; we are more acutely alive when brought into its presence." Downes placed great emphasis on the restorative powers of the painting: "Our horizons expand . . . we take deeper breaths; we are newly heartened for our work in this best of all worlds."[17]

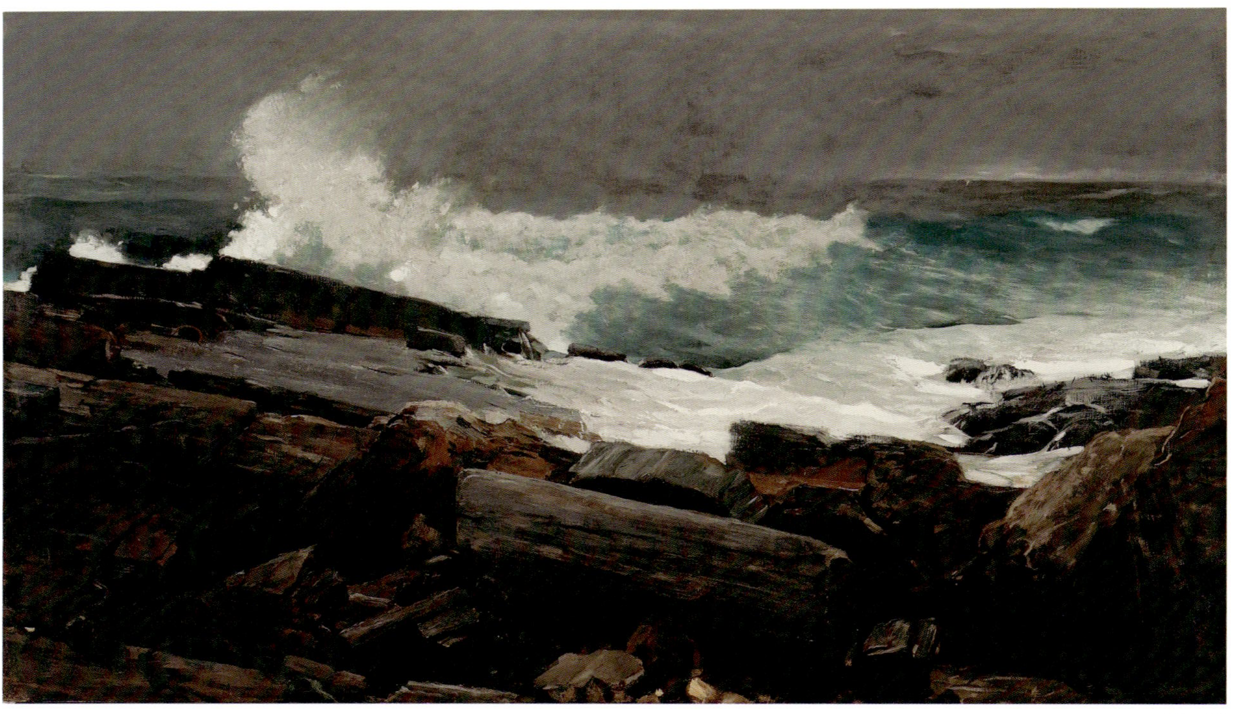

FIG. 10

*Weatherbeaten*, then, was thought to possess therapeutic qualities. A product of the phantasmagoria that was the Gilded Age, *Weatherbeaten*—like *High Cliffs*, *Coast of Maine*, *Winter Coast*, and other paintings by Homer that depict the Cliff Walk at Prouts Neck—filled a need for authentic experience in an uneasy era. As the United States effected a final transition from the face-to-face economy of small-town life to urban, industrial capitalism in the second half of the nineteenth century, the vicissitudes of modern life provoked anxiety. The many promises of modernity, cultural geographer Yi-Fu Tuan has pointed out, left modern men and women feeling socially "orphaned."[18] Worse yet, nebulous feelings of unease led to concrete illness. "Weakened by their new urban lives," writes historian Harvey Green, "spared the rigors of the farm or frontier, vaguely defined illnesses—dyspepsia, neurasthenia—seemed to doom Americans."[19] Homer's answer to the hazards of modernity lay in the close study of the action of the waves as they met the ledge on which he settled and painted.

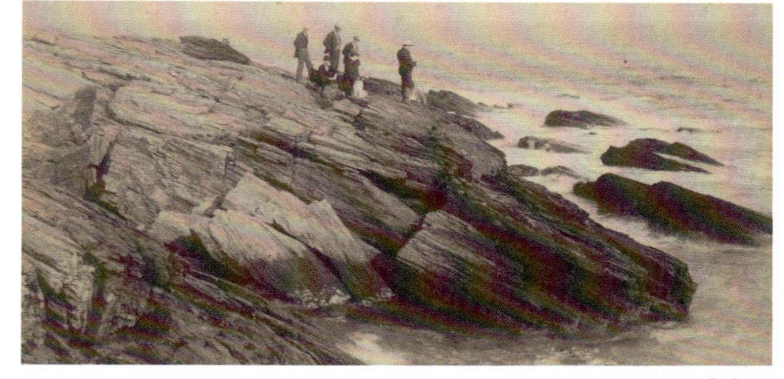

FIG. 11

Geophilia is a time-honored affliction for American painters and their patrons (fig. 11). While earlier generations found their needs served by reading the hand of God or an aesthetic sublime into the rocky outcroppings of the Catskills or the White Mountains, Homer's geology in *Weatherbeaten* is geographically specific and poetically important. The rocks depicted by Homer, mostly schists and gneisses, exhibit a striking lineation that fractures both with and against the "grain," leaving a pleasingly geometric composition and coloration.[20] Period commentators such as Rupert Holland waxed eloquent over Prouts Neck's "sky, sea, and wind-driven foam," but especially "the mighty bulwarks of rock that defend the land from invasion."[21] These large formations are not only muscular guards in Holland's reckoning but serve as characters in Homer's timeless drama of wave striking land. The *Boston Herald*, reviewing *Weatherbeaten* upon exhibition, commented on Homer's ability to capture the "titanic and terrible aspects of nature" and "tremendous, invincible forces" at play in the painting.[22] Beyond the perceived force of the canvas, viewers found a native quality in *Weatherbeaten*. Holland, in particular, found a sense of nation in the littoral, seeing in Homer a "vigor and independence, absolute honesty of presentation, and a profound appreciation of the American atmosphere."[23]

And then there is the gray stripe. *Weatherbeaten* is an extraordinary painting that is of one place, but seemingly of two moments in time. Having tightly painted the breaking wave and employed a spectrum of warm reddish browns to lend the rocks character and subtle mystery, Homer chose to apply an elongated rectangle of gray pigment, rising out of the foam and paralleling the prominent formation at left. A strident gesture, the gray stripe becomes what the literary theorist Roland Barthes has termed a "punctum," the point of connection that draws the eye and begins to unfold an image.[24] Neither land nor water, light nor shadow, the gray stripe is a clarion statement in paint. Earlier in his career, Homer was chastised for such behavior. "If Mr. Homer has adopted the notion that he can put down . . . all that is worth recording, in a half-dozen strokes of his brush, he makes a blunder," wrote the influential critic Clarence Cook in 1868.[25] By 1894, however, Homer was well past middle age, enjoying success, and playing his hand as he chose.

Homer's gray stripe is a statement of artistic independence and authority. Unlike the sly insinuation of *Artists Sketching in the White Mountains*, the wink-and-a-nudge critique of the state of American landscape painting, *Weatherbeaten* is an intense, muscular painting. With great intentionality, Homer worked the canvas until it satisfied his sensibilities and then boldly painted a large, gray window into the future. It is Homer's gift to the art of the coming age, a century that would cultivate abstraction. It is no wonder that the next generation of painters responded to Homer as a kindred spirit, if not a father figure. Robert Henri lionized Homer in his manifesto *The Art Spirit:* "His work would hold a business man straight. He gives the integrity of the oncoming wave. The big strong thing can only be the result of big strong seeing."[26] Henri's student Rockwell Kent took up the theme of fortitude, deriding Homer's early career in favor of the late paintings: "Homer the Realist: why realism was his *job* in his youth! Strong, simple, honest, true, and by the power of those qualities profoundly moving, we claim him proudly as an exemplar of the American character."[27]

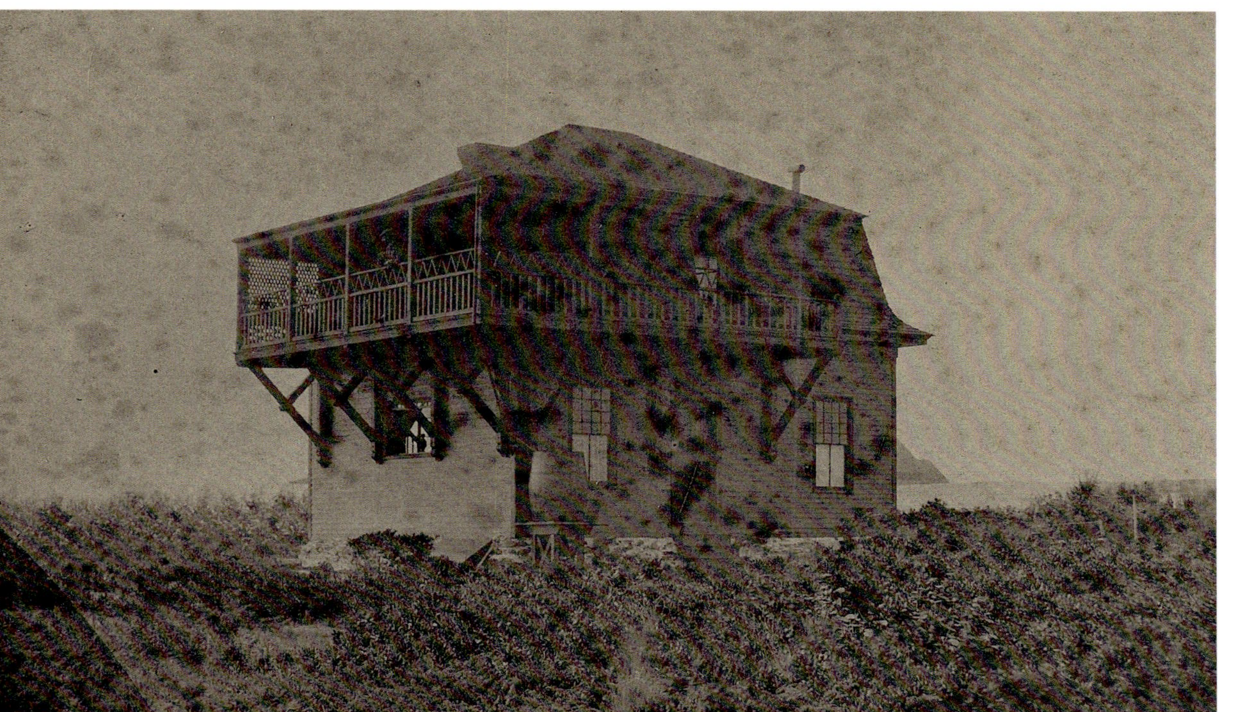

FIG. 12

Simple, strong, honest, American—*Weatherbeaten*, like Homer's other late paintings, foreshadowed the modernist turn to the coast that marked the early twentieth century. The late paintings made Homer the common ancestor to a diverse group of painters who internalized the existential myth of life on the Maine coast and responded to the commitment of a man who would live and work long into the season in a simple studio (fig. 12). *Weatherbeaten* provided an example of the ardent passions perceived as draining away from everyday life and a model for heroism in the modern era.

Homer's commitment to his place, so attractive to the generation that followed his, bordered on the religious. Awash in a sea of faith that was the culture of liberal Protestantism in late-nineteenth-century America, Homer was well aware that the most popular hymn of his era posed the rock as a symbol of Christian faith and fortitude. Although, as art historian Marc Simpson has pointed out, Homer was not one for "organized religious observances." Late in life, Homer wrote to his older brother that "I am so thankful for all 'His Mercies'—that I now write to you. There is certainly some strange power that has some overlook on me & directing my life. That I am in the right place at present there is no doubt."[28] *Weatherbeaten*, capstone of a life lived well, depicts the rocks of Prouts Neck with nuance, reverence, and a timelessness that engenders speculation about what lies over the horizon.

Three paintings, three places, three moments in the career of Winslow Homer—all participate in a poetics of place. These works and the sixteen other watercolors and paintings held by the Portland Museum of Art at the centennial of Homer's death graphically trace the preoccupations of a prodigious talent in a time of great social change. Homer's offerings on canvas, paper, and panel both sublimate and explicate the disquiet of modern life and illustrate how the artist's work came to serve as a fulcrum between Victorian notions of the sentimental and modern visual culture. A tree, a valley, and a rock—all three provide a home for the viewer in an increasingly complicated world, then and now.

## FIGURES

Fig. 1. Napoleon Sarony
*Winslow Homer Taken in New York*, 1880, albumen print.
Bowdoin College Museum of Art, Brunswick, Maine,
Gift of the Homer Family, 1964.69.179.3

Fig. 2. Winslow Homer
*The Army of the Potomac—A Sharp-Shooter on Picket Duty*
from *Harper's Weekly*, 15 November 1862, wood engraving
on wove paper, 9 1/8 x 13 3/4 inches (image).
Gift of Peggy and Harold Osher, 1991.25.95

Fig. 3. Winslow Homer
*The War for the Union 1862—A Cavalry Charge*
from *Harper's Weekly*, 5 July 1862, wood engraving
on wove paper, 13 9/16 x 20 5/8 inches (image).
Gift of Peggy and Harold Osher, 1991.25.131

Fig. 4. Artist unknown
*The Berdan Sharpshooters at Weehawen*
from *Harper's Weekly* (detail), 5 October 1861,
wood engraving on wove paper, 16 x 10 7/8 inches (paper).
Gift of Peggy and Harold Osher, 1991.37.6

Fig. 5. Winslow Homer
Letter from Winslow Homer to George G. Briggs (detail),
19 February 1896.
Archives of American Art.

Fig. 6. Winslow Homer
*Sharpshooter*, 1863, oil on canvas, 12 1/4 x 16 1/2 inches.
Gift of Barbro and Bernard Osher, 1992.41

Fig. 7. Winslow Homer
*August in the Country—The Sea-Shore*
from *Harper's Weekly*, 27 August 1859, wood engraving
on wove paper, 9 1/8 x 13 3/4 inches (image).
Gift of Peggy and Harold Osher, 1991.25.13

Fig. 8. Winslow Homer
*Artists Sketching in the White Mountains*,
1868, oil on panel, 9 1/2 x 15 7/8 inches.
Bequest of Charles Shipman Payson, 1988.55.4

Fig. 9. Winslow Homer
*The Artist in the Country* from *Appletons' Journal*,
19 June 1869, wood engraving on wove paper,
11 1/16 x 7 5/8 inches.
Gift of Peggy and Harold Osher, 1991.25.9

Fig. 10. Winslow Homer
*Weatherbeaten*, 1894, oil on canvas, 28 1/2 x 48 3/8 inches.
Bequest of Charles Shipman Payson, 1988.55.1

Fig. 11. Artist unknown
*Winslow Homer, his dog Sam, his father Charles Savage Homer, Sr., his brother, Charles Savage Homer, Jr., and others watching the ocean from the cliffs, Prouts Neck, Maine*, circa 1895, gelatin silver print.
Bowdoin College Museum of Art, Brunswick, Maine,
Gift of the Homer Family, 1964.69.177.16

Fig. 12. Artist unknown
*Winslow Homer on the Gallery of His Studio, Prouts Neck, Maine*,
circa 1884, gelatin silver print, 4 7/16 x 6 11/16 inches.
Bowdoin College Museum of Art, Brunswick, Maine,
Gift of the Homer Family, 1964.69.153.11

## NOTES

1. William John Loftie, *A Plea for Art at Home* (Philadelphia: Porter and Coates, 1879), 55.

2. Frank Luther Mott, *A History of American Magazines, 1850–1865*, vol. 2 (Cambridge, MA: Harvard University Press, 1957), 475.

3. Drew Gilpin Faust, *This Republic of Suffering: Death and the American Civil War* (New York: Knopf, 2008), 33.

4. Winslow Homer to George Briggs, letter, 19 February 1896, quoted in Marc Simpson, *Winslow Homer: Paintings of the Civil War* (San Francisco: Fine Arts Museums of San Francisco, 1988), 38.

5. John Keegan, *The American Civil War: A Military History* (New York: Knopf, 2009), 46.

6. William Howe Downes, *The Life and Works of Winslow Homer* (Boston: Houghton Mifflin, 1911), 47. Downes recounts the story of the landscape painter Roswell Morse Shurtleff sitting with Homer while the latter worked on the painting. Homer remarked that we would take "not less than sixty dollars, for that was what Harper paid him for a full-page drawing on the wood."

7. Homer's mother writing to her son Arthur, quoted in Gordon Hendricks, *The Life and Work of Winslow Homer* (New York: Harry N. Abrams, 1979), 50.

8. Franklin Kelly, "Winslow Homer and the Deflection of Narrative," *The Magazine Antiques* 148, no. 5 (November 1995): 652–61.

9. Jennifer Greenhill, "Winslow Homer and the Mechanics of Visual Deadpan," *Art History* 32, no. 2 (April 2009): 351–86.

10. Thomas Starr King quoted in Robert McGrath, *Gods in Granite: The Art of the White Mountains of New Hampshire* (Syracuse, NY: Syracuse University Press, 2001), 107.

11. *The Crayon* quoted in Charles O. Vogel, "Wanderings after the Wild and Beautiful: The Life and Career of Benjamin Champney," *Historical New Hampshire* 51, nos. 3 and 4 (Fall/Winter 1996): 80.

12. *Appletons' Journal* (July 10, 1869): 465.

13. "Table-Talk," *Appletons' Journal* (June 19, 1869): 378.

14. Roger Stein, "Picture and Text: The Literary World of Winslow Homer," *Studies in the History of Art* 26: 37–38.

15. Sarah Burns, "Revitalizing the 'Painted Out' North: Winslow Homer, Manly Health, and New England Regionalism in Turn-of-the-Century America," *American Art* (Summer 1995): 25.

16. Frederick W. Morton, "The Art of Winslow Homer," *Brush and Pencil* (1902): 47–48, quoted in ibid., 21.

17. Downes quoted in Sarah Burns, *Inventing the Modern Artist: Art and Culture in Gilded Age America* (New Haven, CT: Yale University Press, 1996), 152.

18. Yi-Fu Tuan, *Escapism* (Baltimore, MD: Johns Hopkins University Press, 1998), 22.

19. Harvey Green, *Fit for America: Health, Fitness, Sport and American Society* (Baltimore, MD: Johns Hopkins University Press, 1986), 321.

20. I would like to thank Eriksen Phenix for identifying the geology of Prouts Neck.

21. Rupert Sargent Holland, *The Story of Prouts Neck* (Prouts Neck, ME: Prouts Neck Association, 1924), 51.

22. *Boston Herald* review quoted in Burns, *Inventing the Modern Artist*, 199.

23. Holland, *Story of Prouts Neck*, 50.

24. Roland Barthes, *Camera Lucida: Reflections on Photography* (New York: Hill and Wang, 1982), 26–27.

25. Clarence Cook quoted in Margaret Conrads, *Winslow Homer and the Critics: Forging a National Art in the 1870s* (Princeton, NJ: Princeton University Press, 2002), 18.

26. Robert Henri quoted in Bruce Robertson, "Perils of the Sea," in William H. Truettner and Roger B. Stein, *Picturing Old New England: Image and Memory* (New Haven, CT: Yale University Press, 1999), 147.

27. Rockwell Kent, *World Famous Paintings* (New York: Wise, 1947), entry 93, unpaginated.

28. Marc Simpson, "Homer's Wine-Dark Seas," in Sophie Levy, ed., *Winslow Homer: Poet of the Seas* (London: Dulwich Picture Gallery, 2006), 33; and Homer quoted in ibid., 33.

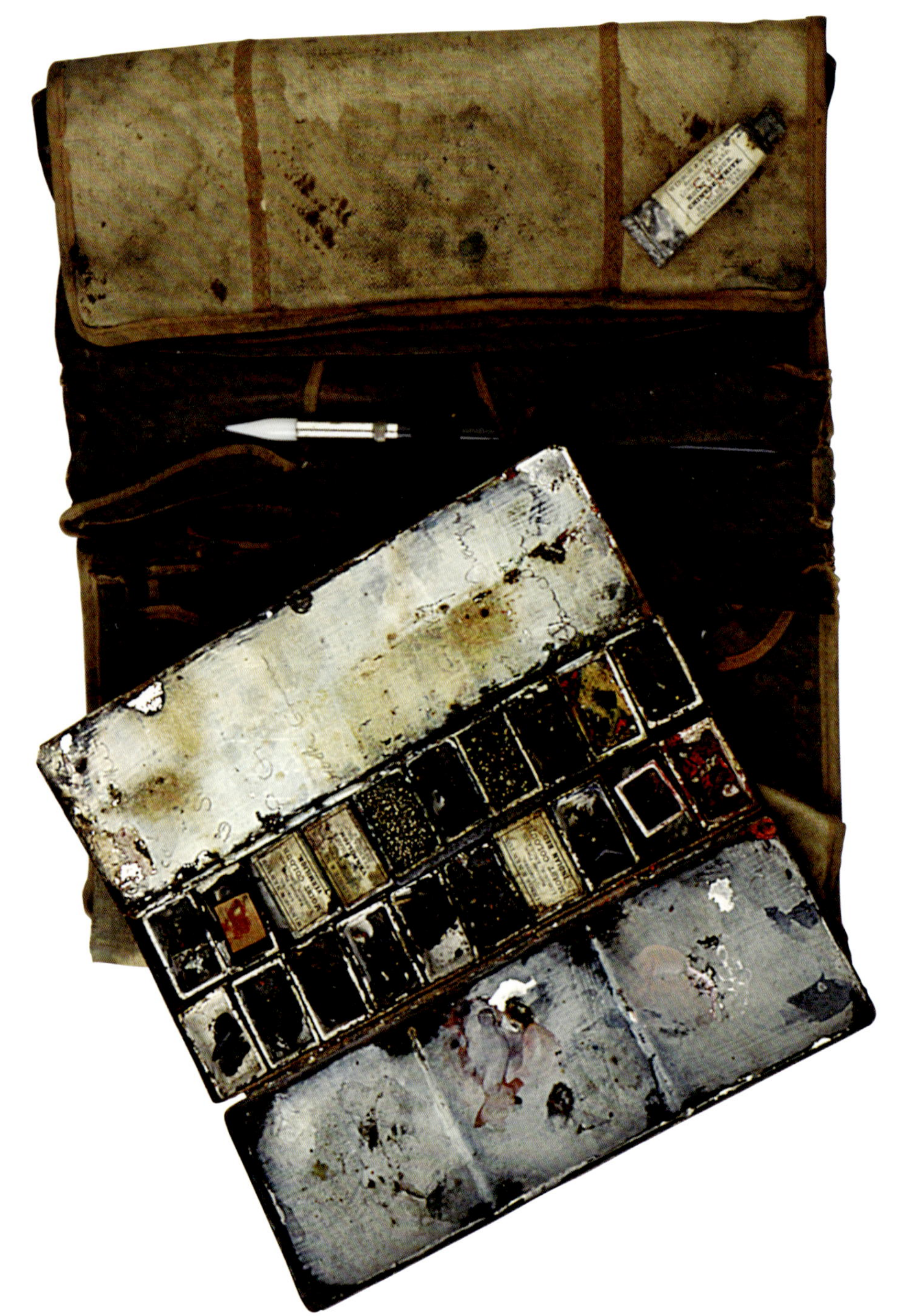

# PLATES

# SHARPSHOOTER

**1863 OIL ON CANVAS**
**12 1/4 x 16 1/2 INCHES**

SIGNED LOWER LEFT: W. HOMER 63
GIFT OF BARBRO AND BERNARD OSHER 1992.41

Closely cropped and devoid of the heroic conventions of nineteenth-century military pomp, Winslow Homer's remarkable debut in oil is a novel painting of a modern war. A product of Homer's firsthand experiences at the front, the inherent tension of the image derives from the painter's ability to essentialize a soldier engaged in the specific act of targeting a chosen adversary. The painting is at once about the universality of faceless death in war and the precision of killing. The discomfort provoked by this contradiction transcends time and elicits a chill today as it did when Homer himself wrote that such activity was "as near murder" as he could imagine.

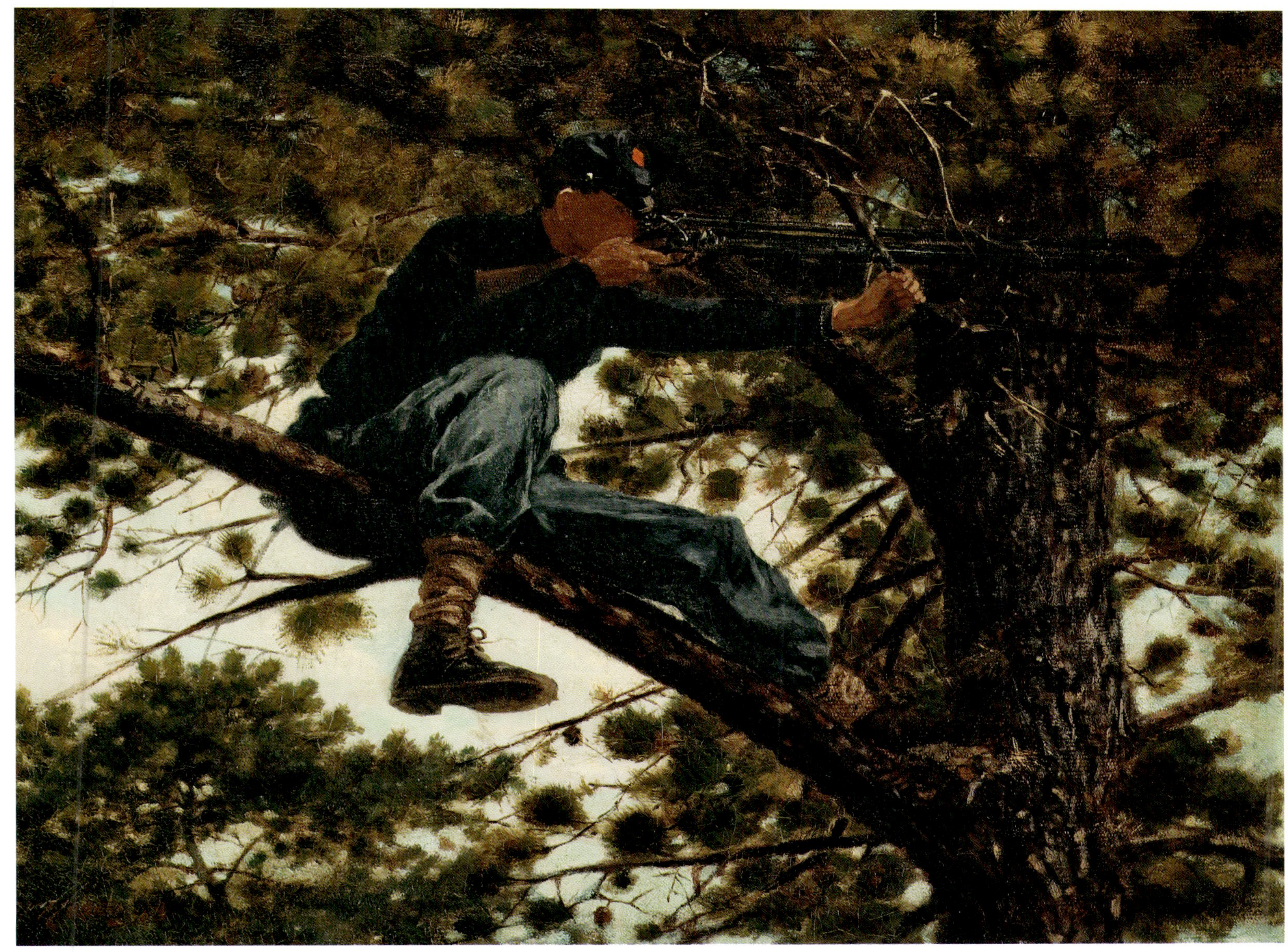

SHARPSHOOTER N° 1992.41

# ARTISTS SKETCHING IN THE WHITE MOUNTAINS

**1868 OIL ON PANEL**
**9 1/2 x 15 7/8 INCHES**

UNSIGNED; INSCRIBED LOWER LEFT: WHITE MTS 1868
BEQUEST OF CHARLES SHIPMAN PAYSON, 1988.55.4

The White Mountains served as a national landscape in the years that followed the Civil War. One of the first regions to engender and exploit a tourist economy in the United States, the towns surrounding the Presidential Range of New Hampshire provided the infrastructure for a generation of artists to capture the view while taking in the fresh air of the country. Painting Mount Washington, the highest peak in the range, came to be considered a rite of passage for artists of every stripe. Homer—ironic in temperament and possessing a keen, self-deprecating sense of humor—took obvious pleasure in depicting himself as last in this queue of plein-air painters as evidenced by the knapsack bearing the inscription "Homer." Although Homer would continue to paint genre subjects throughout the 1870s, the subtle critique evidenced in *Artists Sketching in the White Mountains* would eventually lead him to darker, existential dramas, such as *Weatherbeaten*.

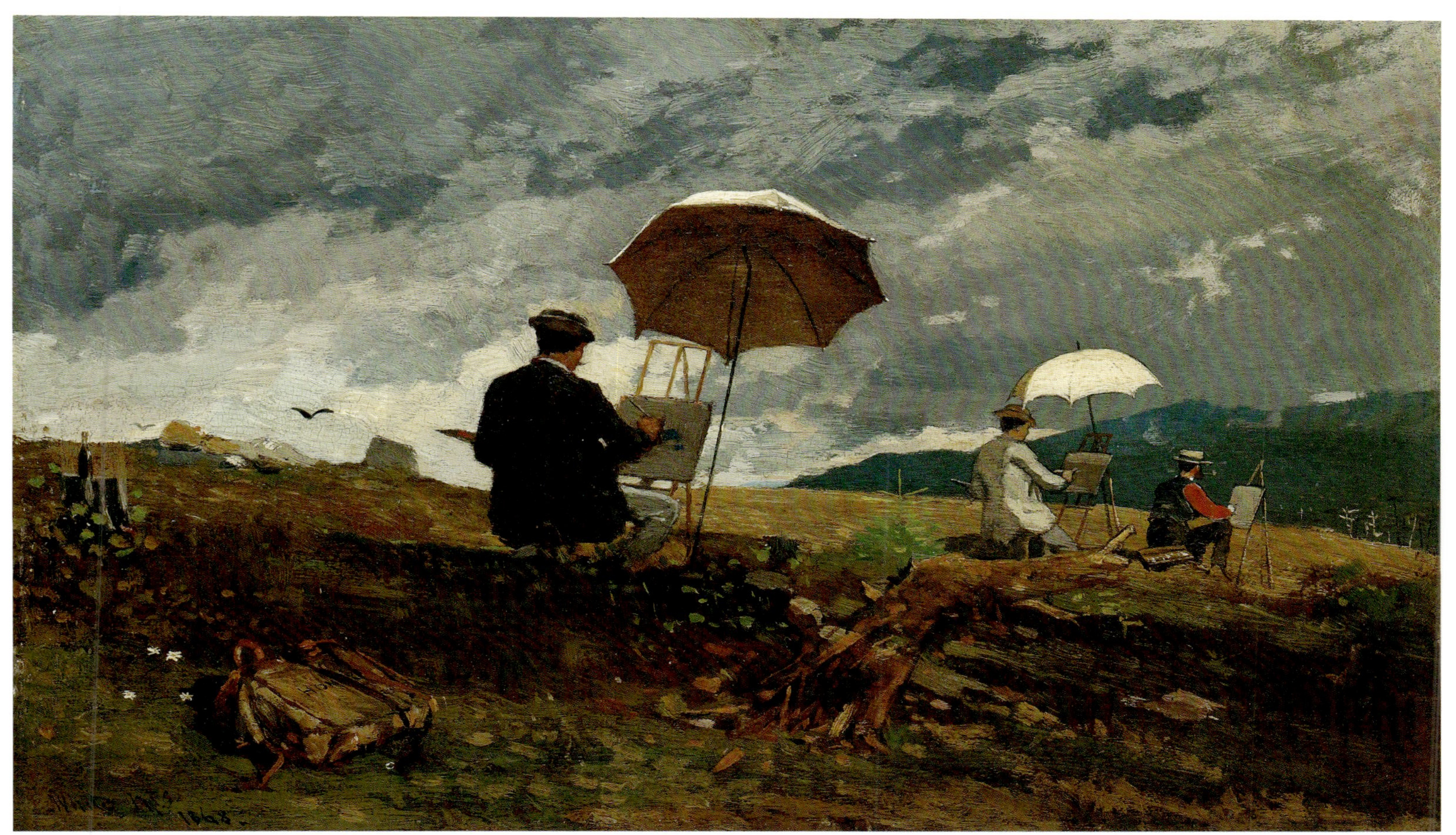

ARTISTS SKETCHING IN THE WHITE MOUNTAINS Nº 1988.55.4

# BOY IN A BOATYARD

**1873 WATERCOLOR AND GOUACHE OVER GRAPHITE ON OFF-WHITE WOVE PAPER**
**7 1/2 x 13 5/8 INCHES**

SIGNED LOWER RIGHT: WINSLOW HOMER 1873
BEQUEST OF CHARLES SHIPMAN PAYSON, 1988.55.5

Homer's genius lay in his ability not only to depict place but also to convey sensation. A hot sun, having bleached the shingles of the boathouse and dried out the barrel staves and wooden casks littering the yard, warms the brow of boy and viewer alike. Remarkably, *Boy in a Boatyard* is the product of Homer's first summer of intensive work in watercolor. Despite the novelty of the medium to the artist, the painting displays a confidence of technique readily seen in the contrast between the bright, drying sail and the moody shadows. The solitary child is a motif that Homer repeated in the 1870s, perhaps as a surrogate for his own desire to retreat from society.

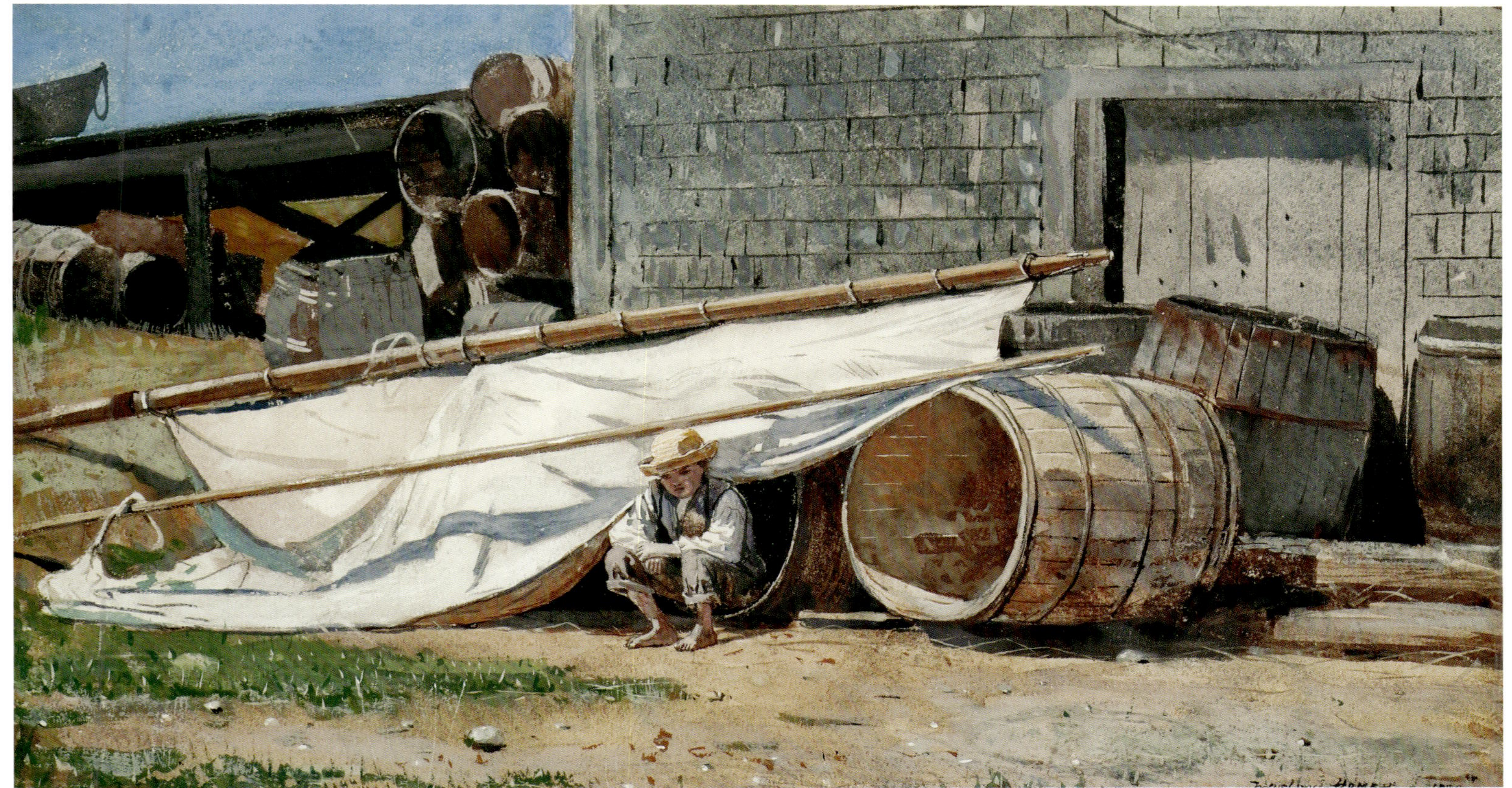

BOY IN A BOATYARD N° 1988.55.5

# TRAPPERS RESTING

**1874 WATERCOLOR ON WOVE PAPER**
**9 3/4 x 13 3/4 INCHES**

SIGNED LOWER RIGHT: HOMER 1874
BEQUEST OF CHARLES SHIPMAN PAYSON, 1988.55.6

Winslow Homer took to the woods and in so doing changed the way Americans looked at their environment. He traveled to the Adirondacks of New York for the first time in 1870, sketching, painting, and producing illustrations of this planned wilderness for the popular journals *Every Saturday* and *Harper's Weekly*. He returned repeatedly and, over time, developed relationships with the hired hands and guides of the North Woods Club. *Trappers Resting* is a document of Homer's passionate interest in the rugged, outdoor life and stands as a wistful icon of traditional labor in an ever-changing and increasingly fast-paced world.

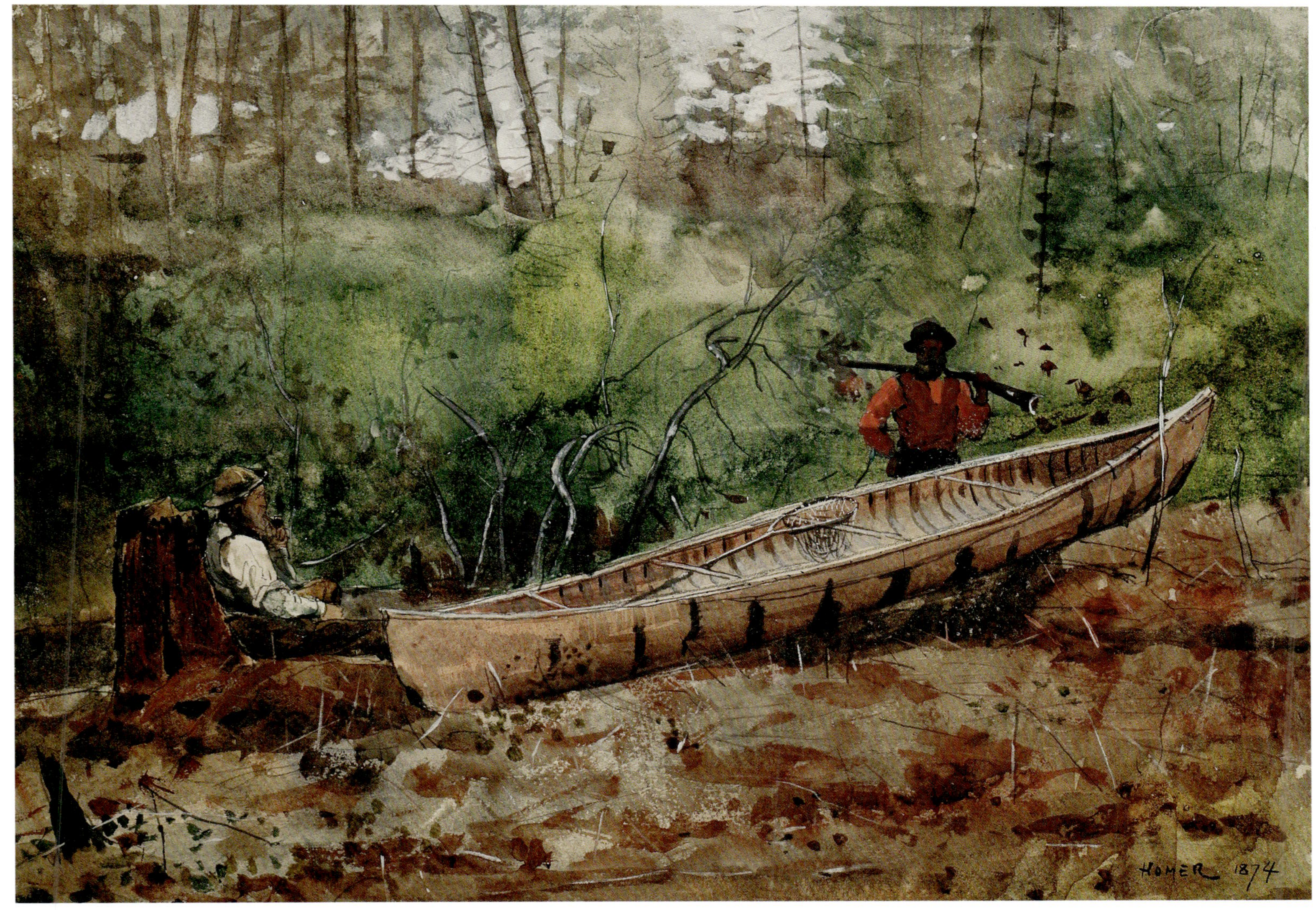


TRAPPERS RESTING N° 1988.55.6

# GIRL SEATED ON HILLSIDE OVERLOOKING THE WATER

**1878 WATERCOLOR AND GRAPHITE ON PAPER**
**8 3/4 x 11 5/16 INCHES**

SIGNED LOWER LEFT: 1878 WINSLOW HOMER
GIFT OF LILY W. RUSSELL AND FAMILY, 1998.28

Images of children enjoyed great currency in the last quarter of the nineteenth century. As the United States celebrated its centennial and prepared to step out onto the world stage as an international power, nostalgic views of rural life and the innocence of youth served as visual substitutes for conversations about change and modernity. Painted in 1878 during Homer's stay at Houghton Farm—the summer home of Lawson and Lucy Valentine in Montville, New York—this scene depicts a girl on the cusp of adolescence, singular and alone, staring into a mirrorlike lake. Her head is turned away from the picture plane, hiding the child's features and rendering her universal. She is lent character by a bright red ribbon in her long braid—the small flash of color a device favored by Homer. A symbol of the young nation, she pensively looks into a bright, but opaque, future.

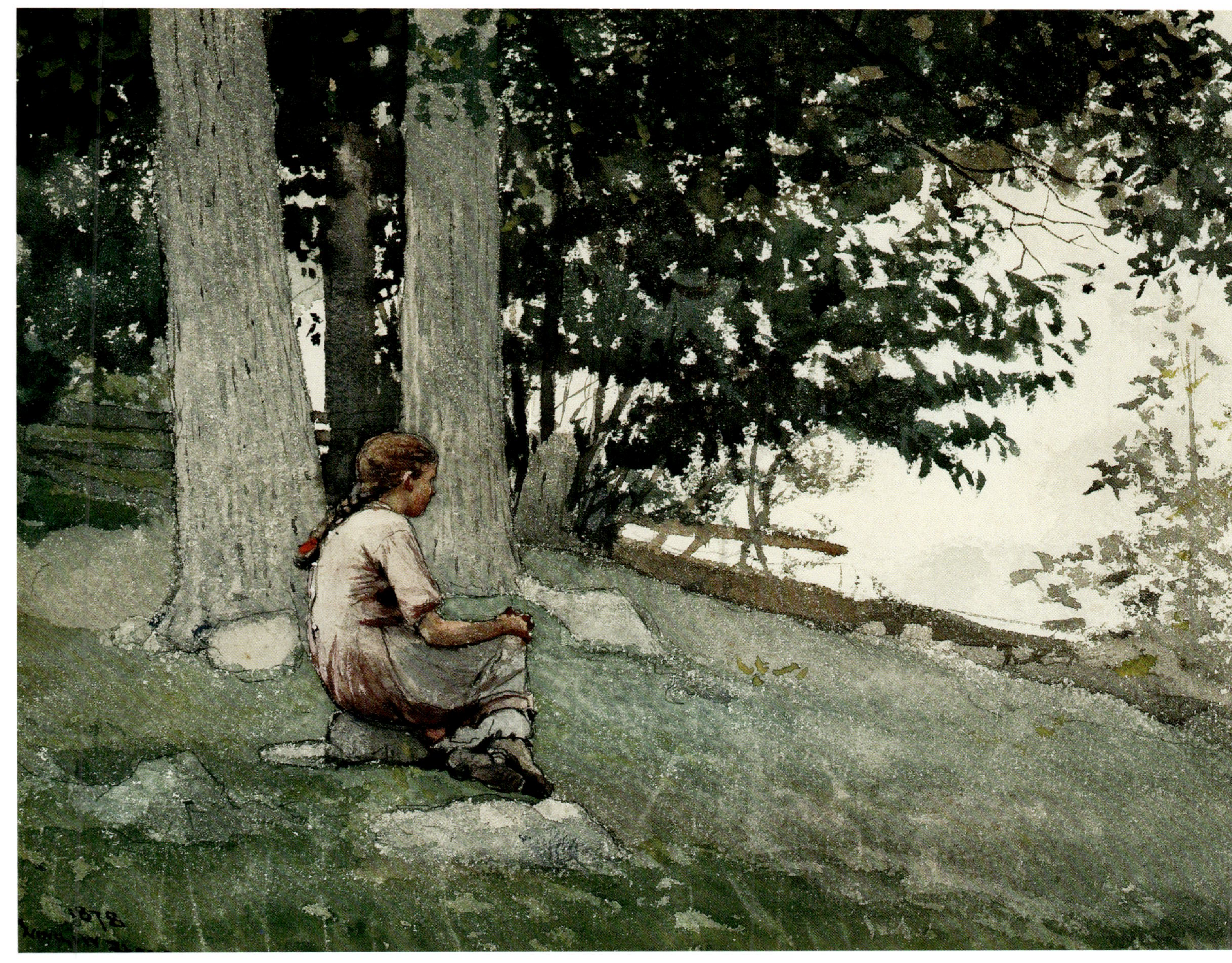

GIRL SEATED ON HILLSIDE OVERLOOKING THE WATER N° 1998.28

# WINDY DAY, CULLERCOATS

**1881 GRAPHITE AND GOUACHE ON TAN LAID PAPER**
**11 3/16 x 20 1/4 INCHES**

SIGNED LOWER LEFT: WINSLOW HOMER 1881
BEQUEST OF CHARLES SHIPMAN PAYSON, 1988.55.15

Homer's sense of bravado, previously restrained by his fondness for irony, is on full display in *Windy Day, Cullercoats*. The product of the artist's eighteen-month stay on the North Sea, drawings such as this reflect Homer's search for authentic experience in everyday life. Impressed by the hearty women of this fishing village, Homer sketched his model from a low angle, creating a dramatic sense of perspective that renders the figure heroic. Homer's refined eye can be seen in how he delineates the arch of the woman's back, leaning away from the wind just as the mast of the vessel strains against the sail. Her billowing apron demonstrates the force of nature buffeting the fleet heading to sea in the background. With sleeves rolled up and market basket at the hip, Homer's figure is muscular, capable, and self-contained in the face of a rugged and challenging environment. Homer's technical genius is revealed not only in his forceful draftsmanship but also in his exquisite use of negative space.

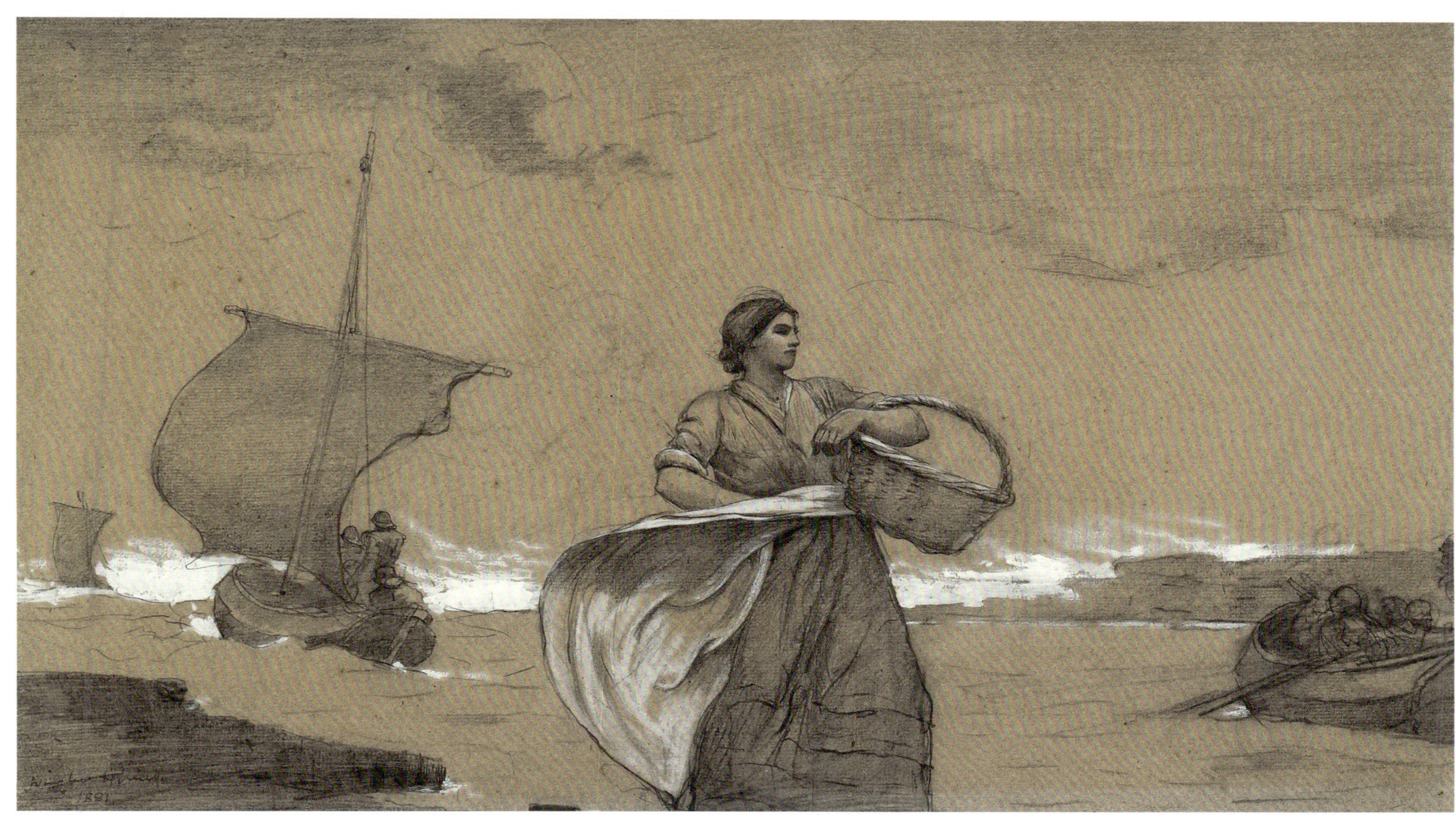

WINDY DAY, CULLERCOATS N° 1988.55.15

# THE BREAKWATER, CULLERCOATS

**1882 WATERCOLOR ON IVORY WOVE PAPER**
**13 1/4 x 19 3/4 INCHES**

SIGNED LOWER RIGHT: WINSLOW HOMER 1882
BEQUEST OF CHARLES SHIPMAN PAYSON, 1988.55.16

Homer remained fascinated by the women of Cullercoats throughout his stay in the English fishing village. Men, when they appear at all, are consigned to supporting roles, backs turned, carrying gear, and lurking in the shadows. Homer's ability to capture the dignity and strength of these fishermen's wives speaks to his profound sensitivity to the timeless quality of their lives. Looking closely at the scene through Homer's eyes, it is hard to tell if the women or the breakwater is better equipped to withstand the forces of the North Sea.

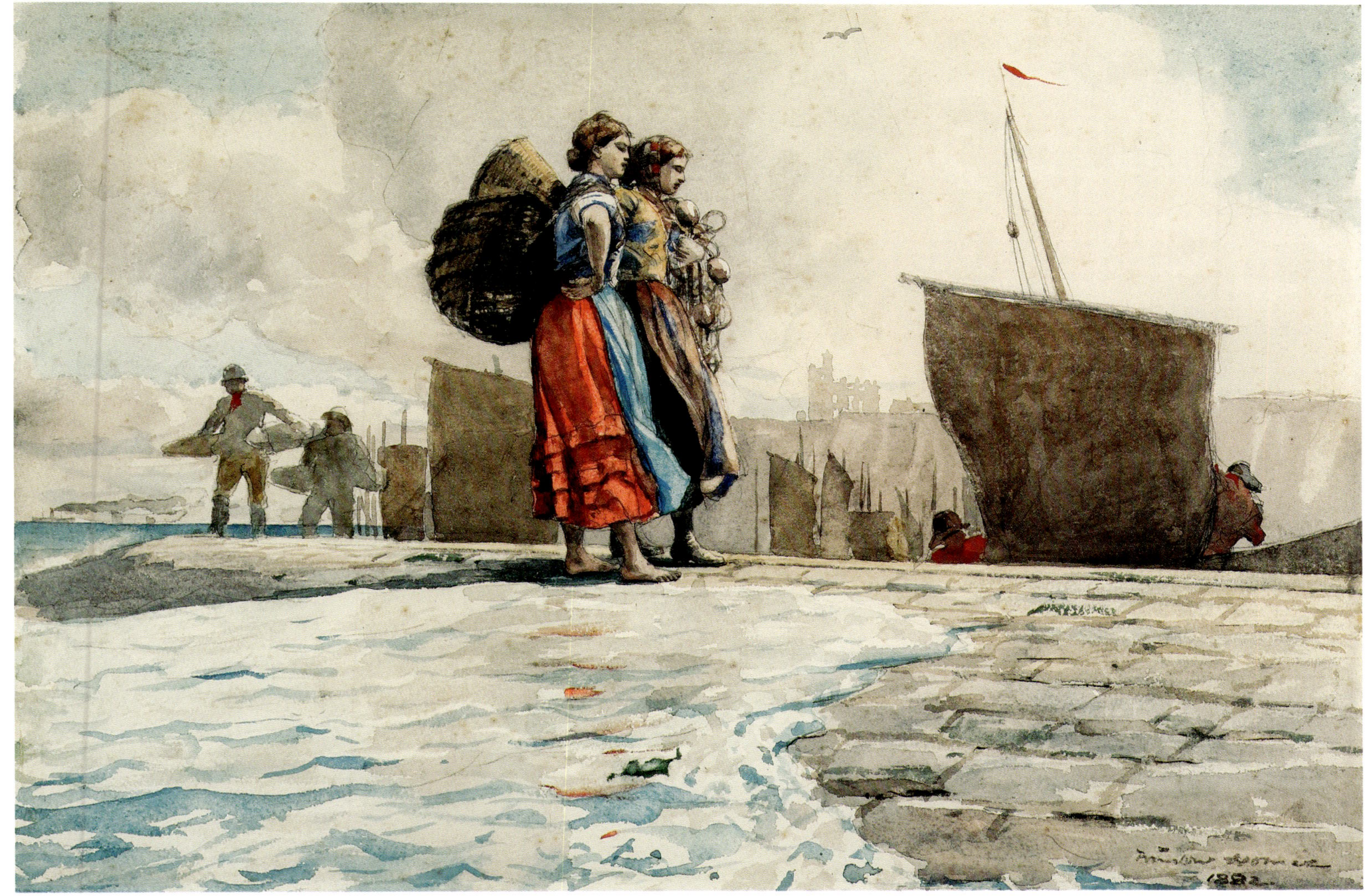

THE BREAKWATER, CULLERCOATS N° 1988.55.16

# LOOKING OUT TO SEA, CULLERCOATS

**1882 WATERCOLOR ON PAPER**
**13 3/4 x 20 INCHES**

SIGNED LOWER RIGHT: WINSLOW HOMER 1882
BEQUEST OF CHARLES SHIPMAN PAYSON, 1988.55.17

Homer admired the constancy of character found in the women of Cullercoats. Time and time again, he sketched the heroic strength and capability of these English fishermen's wives as archetypes of traditional female labor. The prominent baskets and fishing nets, age-old symbols of industry, sharply contrast with the frivolity of parasols and croquet mallets found in the hands of Homer's American women of the 1870s. The ancient narrative of taking sustenance from the ocean is robustly captured in these large watercolors, though Homer is quick to remind the viewer that modern life lurks on the horizon in the form of a small, dark steamship.

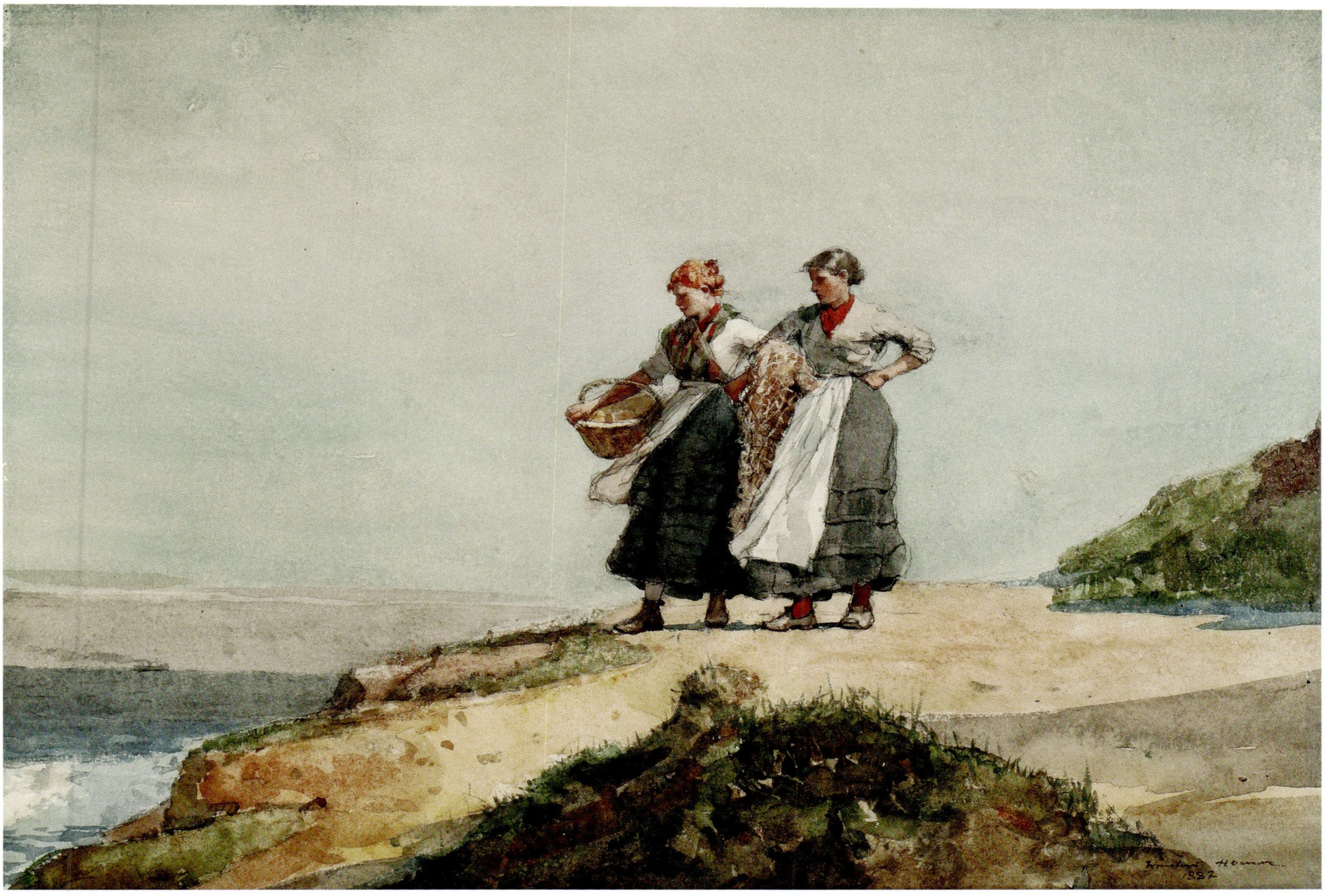

LOOKING OUT TO SEA, CULLERCOATS N° 1988.55.17

# TAKING AN OBSERVATION

**CIRCA 1886 OIL ON PANEL**
**15 1/4 x 24 INCHES**

UNSIGNED
BEQUEST OF CHARLES SHIPMAN PAYSON, 1988.55.3

Winslow Homer learned his craft as an illustrator, employing lessons perfected in the commercial world throughout his career. The monochromatic palette of *Taking an Observation* is a nod to Homer's days of producing images in the service of text, for painting *en grisaille* was a popular technique used by artists communicating with engravers in the burgeoning publishing industry. This striking study in gray, however, is a purely aesthetic choice, as Homer executed the scene to be a decorative panel for the cabin of his brother's sailing yacht.

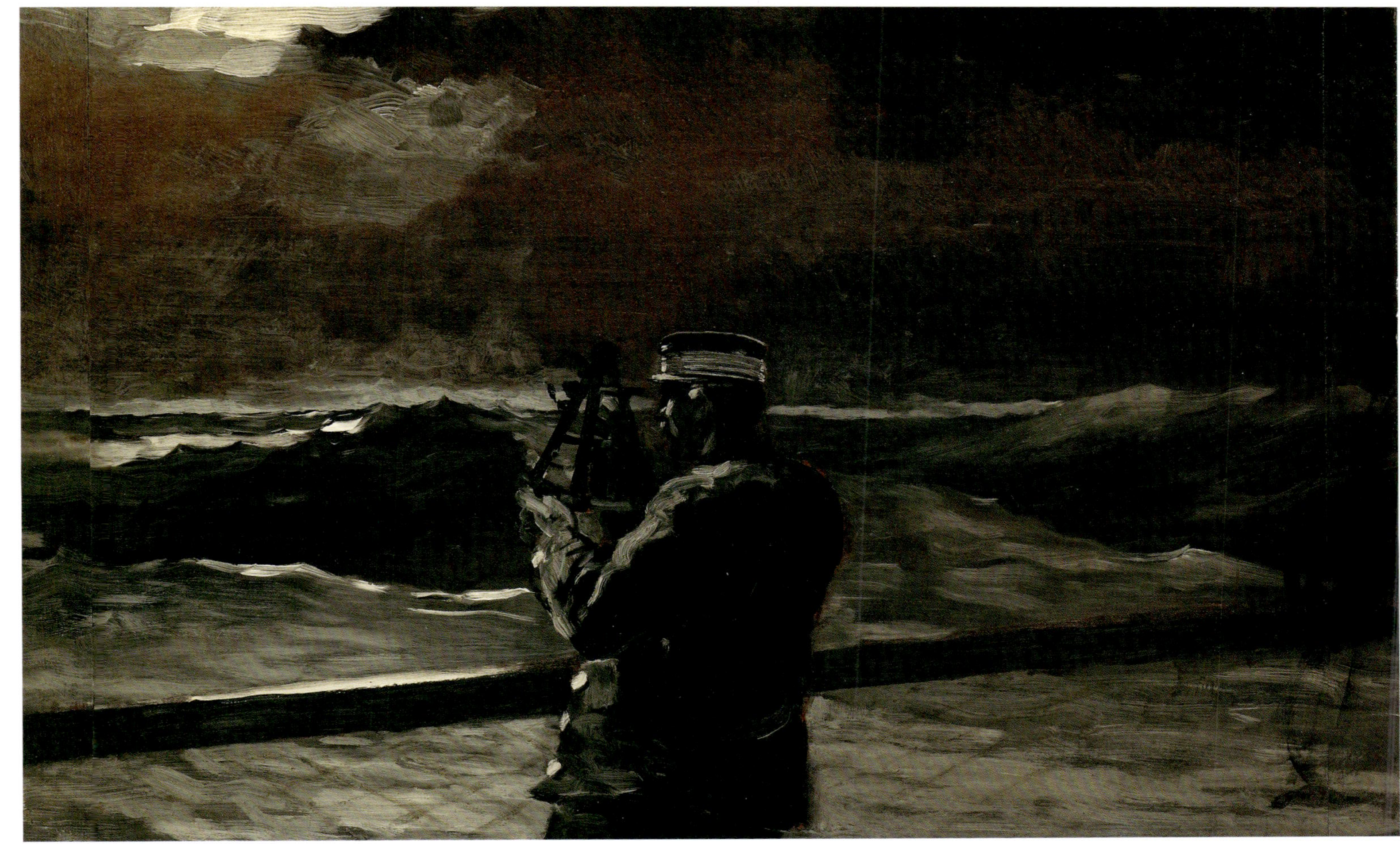

TAKING AN OBSERVATION N° 1988.55.3

# BRINGING IN THE NETS

**1887 WATERCOLOR ON PAPER**
**13 3/4 x 21 1/4 INCHES**

SIGNED LOWER LEFT: WINSLOW HOMER 1887
SIGNED LOWER RIGHT: WINSLOW HOMER
BEQUEST OF CHARLES SHIPMAN PAYSON, 1988.55.14

A contrast to Homer's strong and jaunty women of Cullercoats is the solitary fisherman of *Bringing in the Nets*. Painted some five years after Homer's return from his English sojourn, this American scene but faintly echoes his earlier explorations of the nobility of taking sustenance from the sea. Whereas Homer depicted his female models from Cullercoats in capable poses on promontories, in this later work, the fisherman is up to his knees in high tide, bent over by his burden, and all but tangled himself in marsh grass. Great houses on the horizon reinforce the man's station in life, in contrast to the earlier watercolors, wherein Homer depicted the simple folk of Cullercoats as a natural royalty.

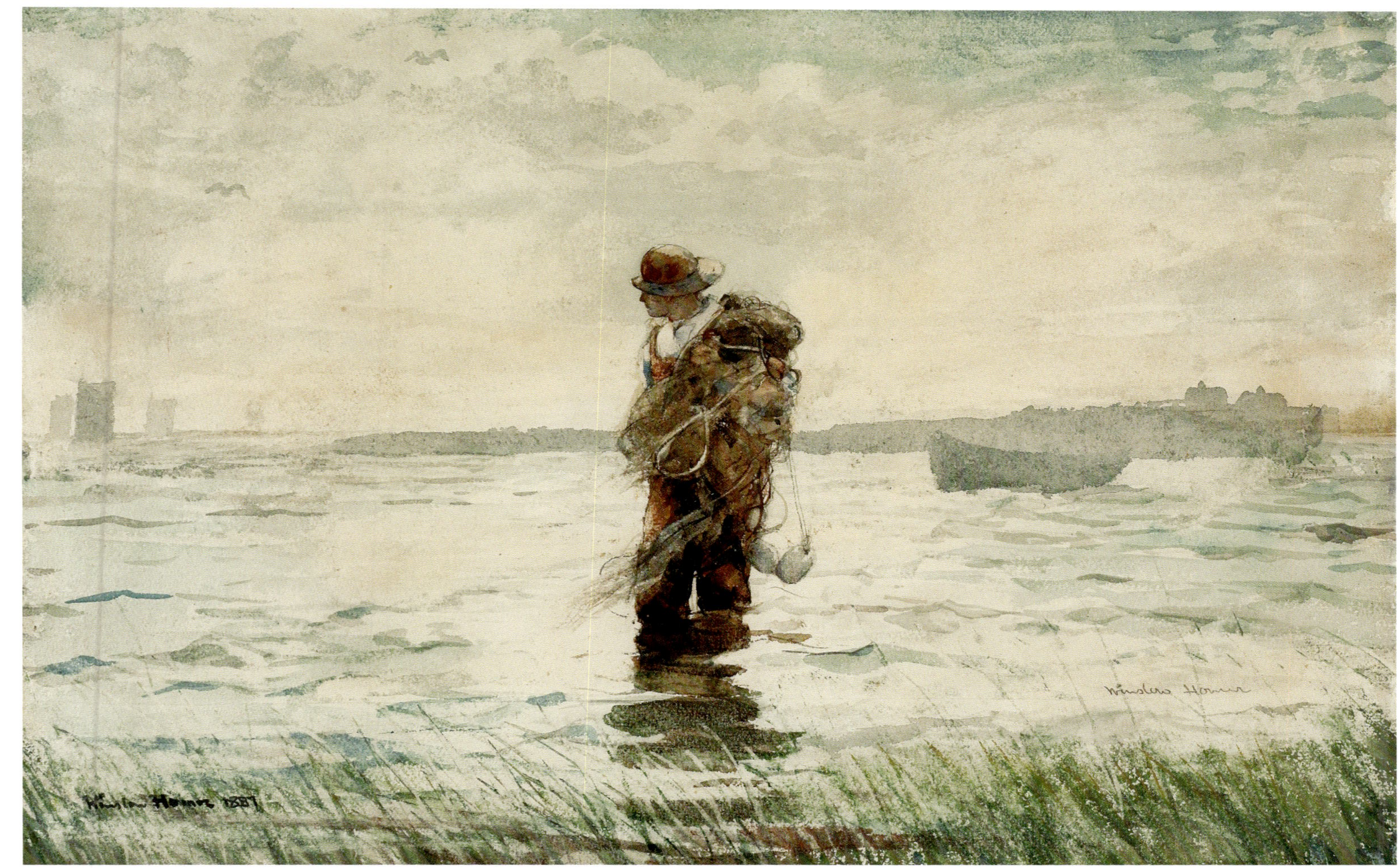

BRINGING IN THE NETS N° 1988.55.14

# THE GUIDE

**1889 WATERCOLOR ON IVORY WOVE PAPER**
**13 3/4 x 19 1/2 INCHES**

SIGNED LOWER LEFT: WINSLOW HOMER 1889
BEQUEST OF CHARLES SHIPMAN PAYSON, 1988.55.8

Rufus Wallace, a hired hand at the North Woods Club in Minerva, New York, modeled for Homer for almost twenty-five years. Wallace, often depicted alongside a younger model to suggest intergenerational camaraderie, is seen here in advanced age and alone. He is the light-struck protagonist in the center of a dark and foreboding scene. But for the shaft of sunshine that illuminates his face, paddle, and wake, Wallace would recede into the forest, a natural man in an urban age. Although Wallace himself is an archetype, his vessel provides an instant sense of place. The guide boat, perfected in the mid-nineteenth century, provided a sturdy and lightweight means to navigate the Adirondack's rivers and lakes. As the region evolved into a controlled wilderness for Americans pursuing the experience of nature as a cure for the perceived dangers of modern life, hours in a guide boat and the company of rugged individuals like Wallace were widely held to be therapeutic pastimes.

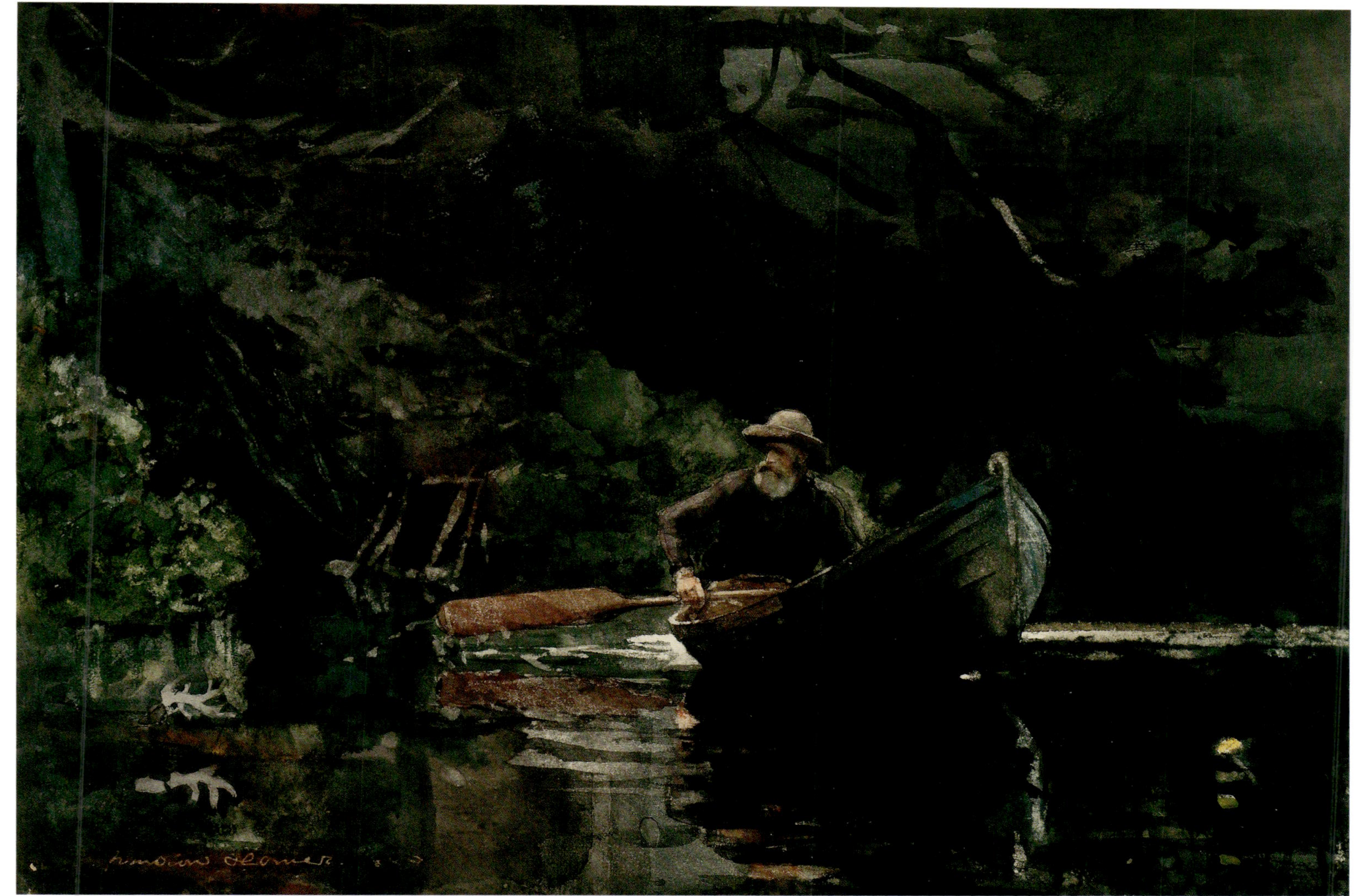

THE GUIDE N° 1988.55.8

# LEAPING TROUT

**1889 WATERCOLOR ON PAPER**
**14 1/16 x 20 1/16 INCHES**

SIGNED LOWER RIGHT: WINSLOW HOMER 1889
BEQUEST OF CHARLES SHIPMAN PAYSON, 1988.55.7

Winslow Homer's credentials as a sportsman were well established by the time he returned to the Adirondacks in 1889. A seasoned and savvy fisherman, he had experience angling around the world and particularly enjoyed casting for brook trout with his brother Charles at the North Woods Club in Minerva, New York. Homer tarried at the club in 1889, staying for almost four months. The artist's firsthand knowledge of the feeding habits of trout and his keen ability to depict a fish rising to take the fly have made his Adirondack scenes canonical images in the history of American sport.

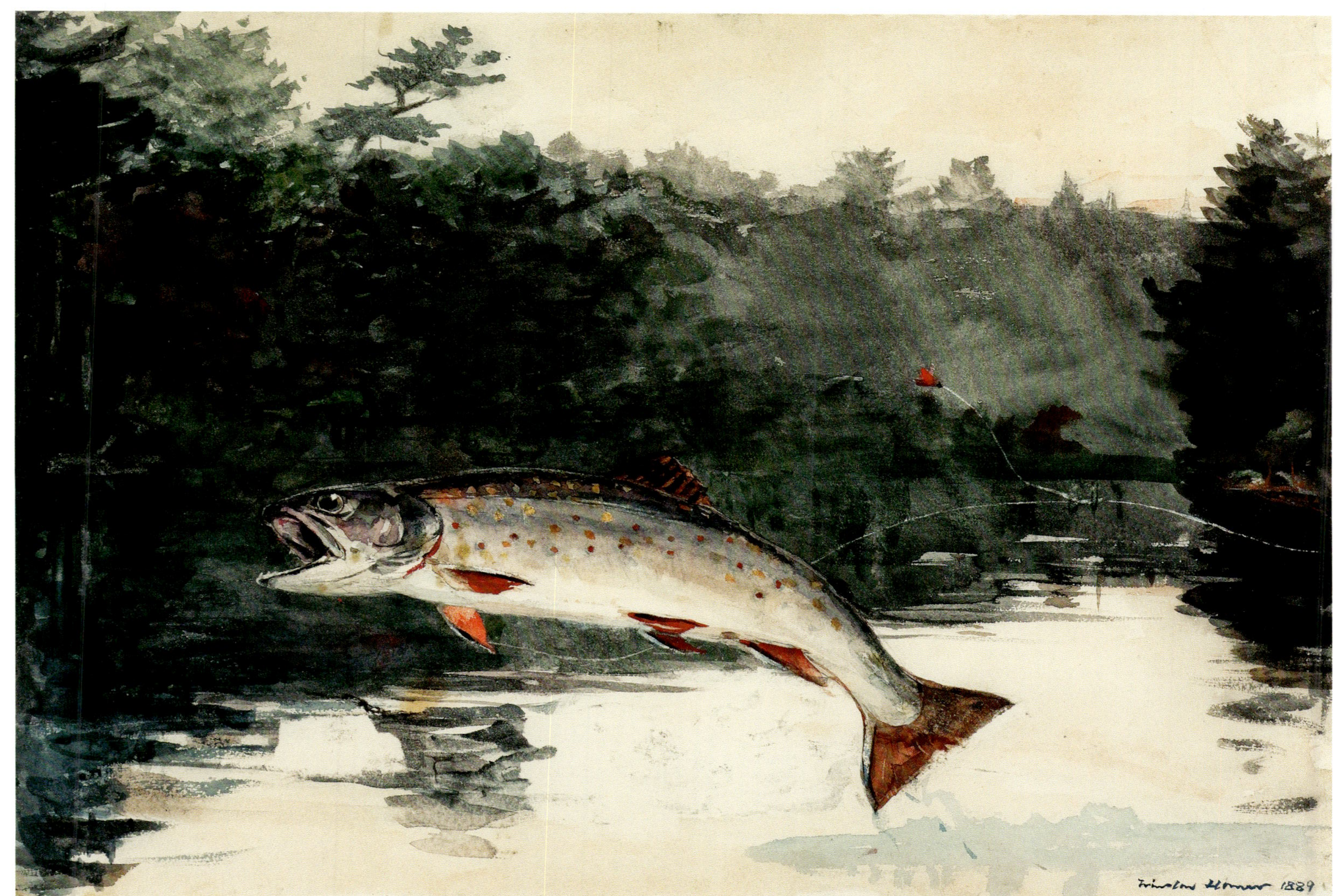


LEAPING TROUT N° 1988.55.7

# AN UNEXPECTED CATCH

**1890 WATERCOLOR ON PAPER**
**11 1/2 x 19 3/4 INCHES**

SIGNED LOWER LEFT: HOMER 90
BEQUEST OF CHARLES SHIPMAN PAYSON, 1988.55.9

Winslow Homer adhered to the color theories of Michel Eugène Chevreul throughout his career. In 1860, Homer's brother Charles gave him an English translation of the famous text by the French chemist. Homer called the book his "Bible," annotating the volume and dating his comments in 1873, 1882, and 1884. Canonical or not, Chevreul sought to document and describe the experience of color, focusing attention on the influence of light and emphasizing the ability of contrasting colors to catch and hold the eye of the beholder—here, witness the way in which the red fly dazzles the viewer, just as it proves fatally tempting to the unwanted sunfish.

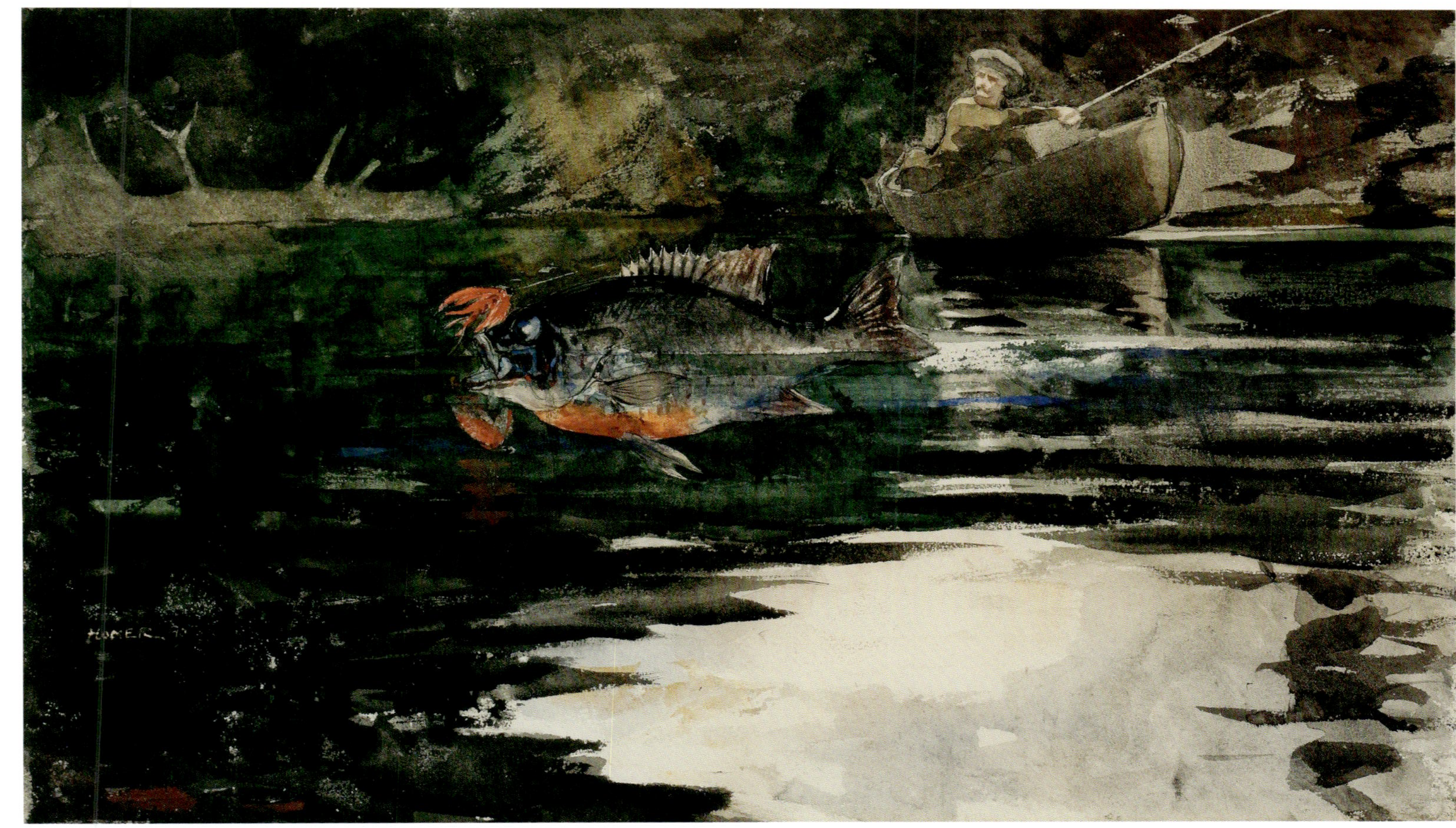


AN UNEXPECTED CATCH N° 1988.55.9

# GUIDE CARRYING A DEER

**1891 WATERCOLOR ON IVORY WOVE PAPER**
**14 x 20 1/16 INCHES**

INSCRIBED UPPER RIGHT: TO C. S. H., JR.,
WITH THE COMPTS. OF WINSLOW HOMER CHRISTMAS 1891
BEQUEST OF CHARLES SHIPMAN PAYSON, 1988.55.10

Seasons and cycles abound in *Guide Carrying a Deer.* The autumnal colors of the hillside scrub explicitly mark the calendar, while cleanly felled trees note the changes brought by man to the Adirondacks. Homer's poignant choices of an adolescent guide and a young buck emphasize the artist's ability to distill the vicissitudes of life and death into a single image. A Christmas gift to his brother, the sketch itself may have been a reference to Homer's own sense of the passage of time. Although Homer went on to develop this study into a large oil painting, the spontaneity of watercolor lends the composition drama and authenticity. The guide's left foot seemingly steps off the paper, setting up a perception of youthful vigor overcoming the awkward uphill carry. Twin peaks on the ominous and distant ridgeline suggest the rhythm and spring of muscle and sinew as the guide hefts his burden.

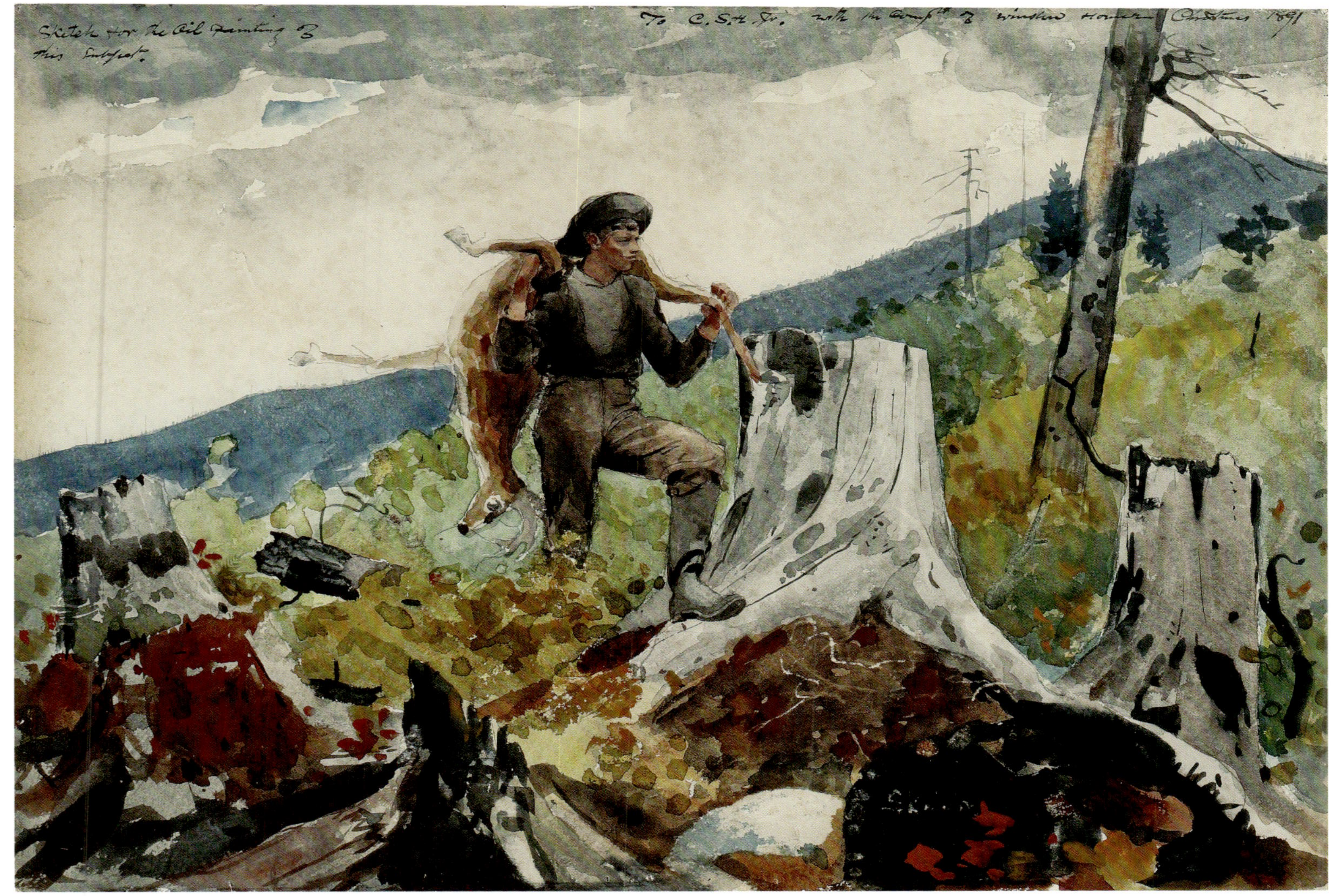


GUIDE CARRYING A DEER N° 1988.55.10

# PICKEREL FISHING

**1892 WATERCOLOR ON WOVE PAPER**
**11 1/4 x 20 INCHES**

SIGNED LOWER RIGHT: WINSLOW HOMER 1892 (SKETCH)
BEQUEST OF CHARLES SHIPMAN PAYSON, 1988.55.11

As a student of the color theories of the French chemist Michel Eugène Chevreul, Homer well knew the dazzling impact of the red pigment at the epicenter of *Pickerel Fishing*. Homer freely employs blues and greens in the lush composition to create a watery background for the striking scene of blood in the water as the large fish bleeds out its gills and stains the lake around the guide boat. Sanguinary and beautiful, this work exhibits Homer's frank assessment of sport, nature, and the circle of life.

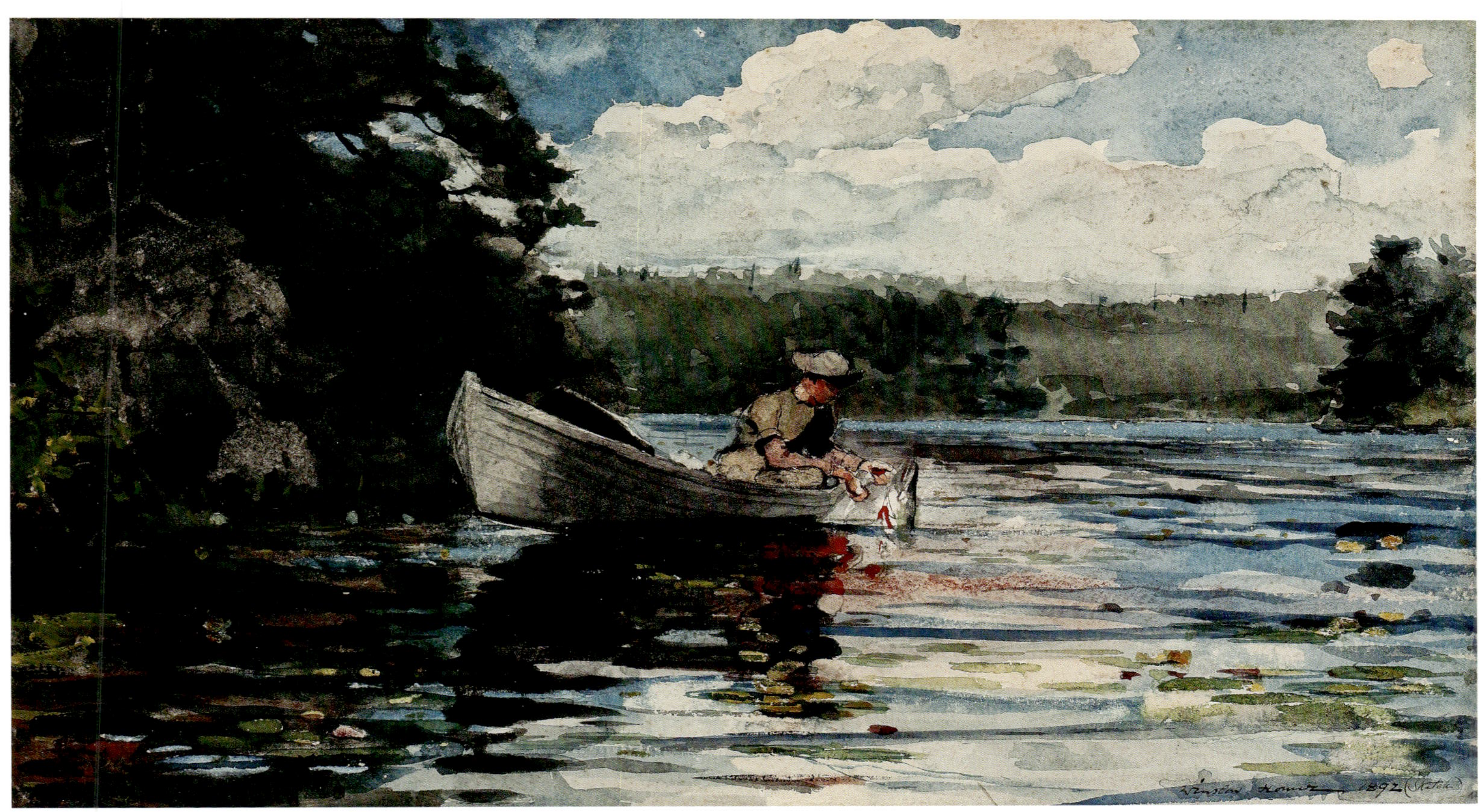


PICKEREL FISHING N° 1988.55.11

# WEATHERBEATEN

**1894 OIL ON CANVAS**
**28 1/2 x 48 3/8 INCHES**

SIGNED LOWER RIGHT: HOMER 94
BEQUEST OF CHARLES SHIPMAN PAYSON, 1988.55.1

Late in life, Homer turned his hand to the timeless drama of the Atlantic Ocean. His paintings of the 1890s are archetypes of close observation and direct experience, the product of a decade of living and painting at Prouts Neck. These dark paintings—forceful, poetic, and exhibiting an intimate knowledge of the sea in its many moods—redirected popular attention to the coast and repositioned New England as a final frontier. With the American West declared closed by historian Frederick Jackson Turner the previous year, Homer's *Weatherbeaten* is an existential manifesto about the challenges of nature in the modern world. The wilderness, long a westerly ideal in the collective memory of the United States, is relocated to a timeless place where the waves of the Atlantic strike the Eastern Seaboard.

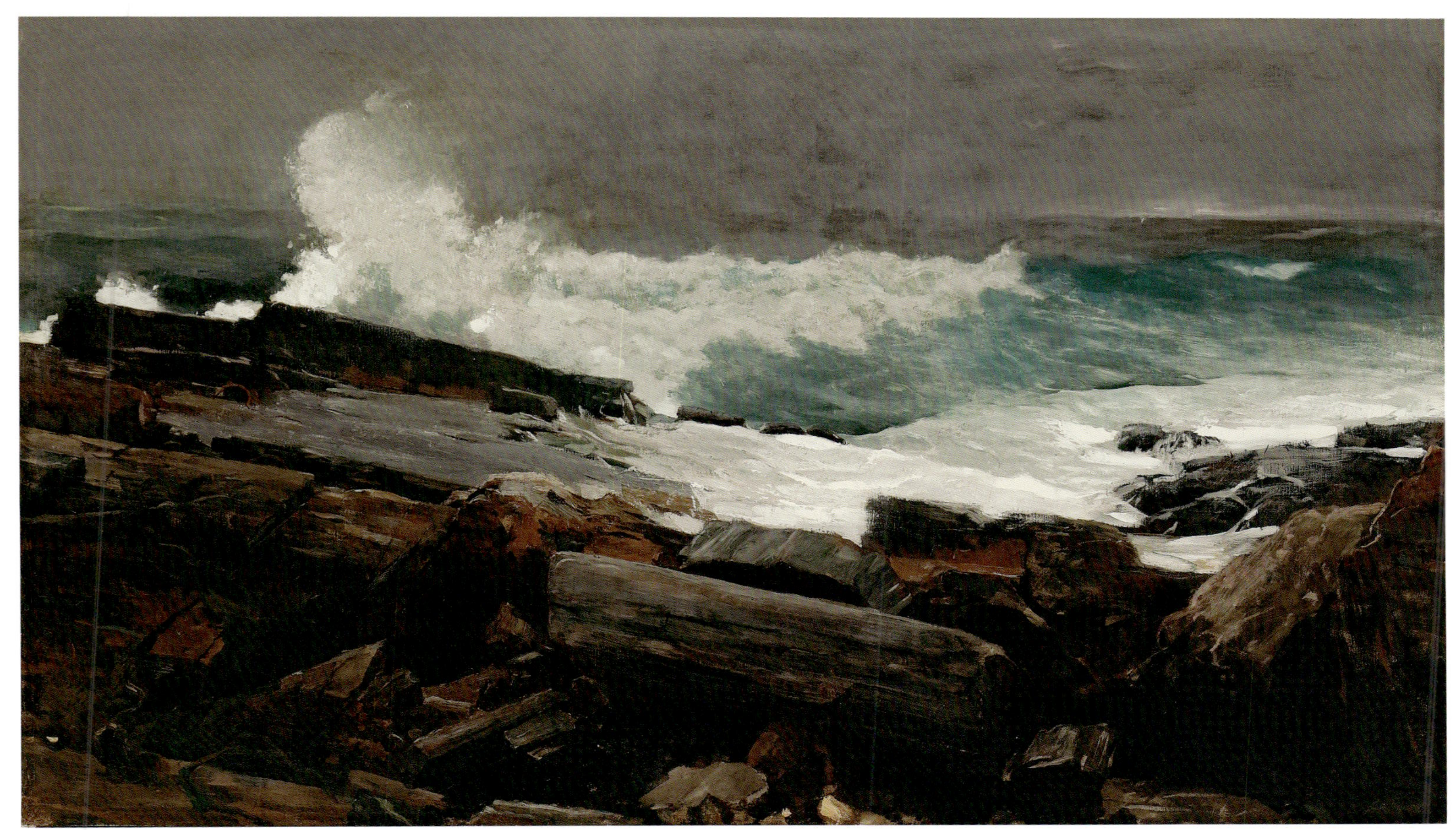

WEATHERBEATEN N° 1988.55.1

# TWO MEN IN A CANOE

**1895 WATERCOLOR ON GRAY LAID PAPER**
**14 x 20 INCHES**

SIGNED LOWER RIGHT: WINSLOW HOMER P. Q. CANADA, SEPTR, 1895
BEQUEST OF CHARLES SHIPMAN PAYSON, 1988.55.12

Homer's ability to depict quiescence rivaled his skill at capturing the raw force of nature on display in works such as *Weatherbeaten*. Painted on one of Homer's late visits to Canada, *Two Men in a Canoe* is a study in subtlety and technique. The artist employs the paper itself to color both water and sky, splitting earth and heaven with deft, minimal brush strokes to create the shore out of misty wash. The canoe's silent wake and the whip of the fishing line—both rendered in pure white gouache—testify to Homer's ability to produce watercolors that all but make sound.

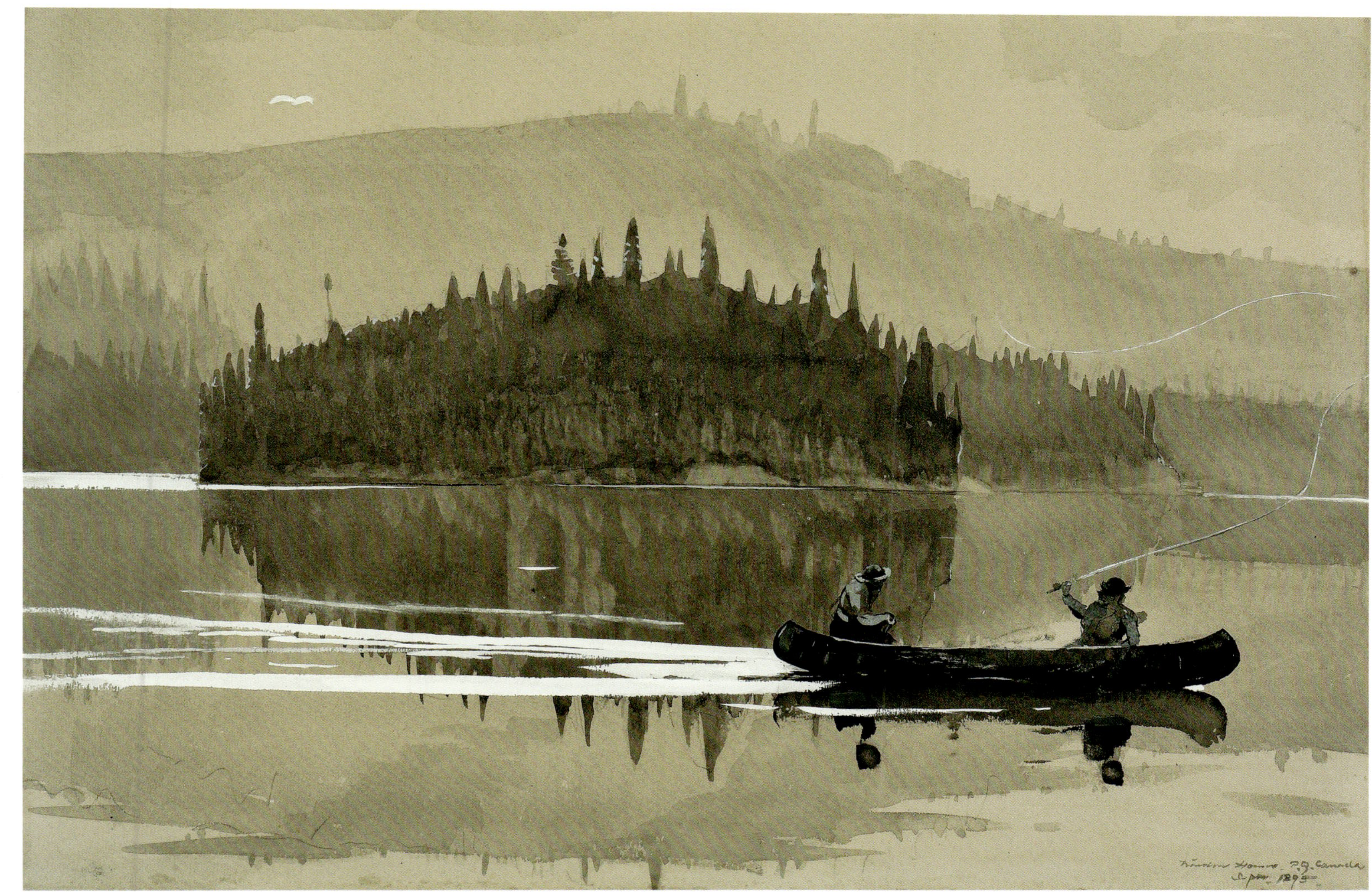

TWO MEN IN A CANOE N° 1988.55.12

# PORTRAIT OF BENJAMIN JOHNSON LANG

**1895 GRAPHITE ON WOVE PAPER**
**16 x 13 3/8 INCHES**

SIGNED LOWER LEFT: W.H. APRIL 19, 1895
GIFT OF WILLIAM D. HAMILL, 1991.19.3

Winslow Homer shared confidences with his sister-in-law Martha, known as Mattie. Married to Homer's brother Charles, Mattie preserved their correspondence, thus providing a rare glimpse at the artist's social life at Prouts Neck, in Boston, and in New York. This pencil portrait is of Mattie's great friend Benjamin Johnson Lang (1837–1909) and, when combined with Homer's letter to Mattie, serves as a document of the tight-knit Homer family. Lang—a prominent Boston symphony conductor, pianist, and organist—sat for Homer on April 19, 1895, in the musician's studio on Newbury Street in Boston. Homer sent the sketch to Mattie the following day as a token of his affection, along with a detailed letter describing his fidgety sitter.

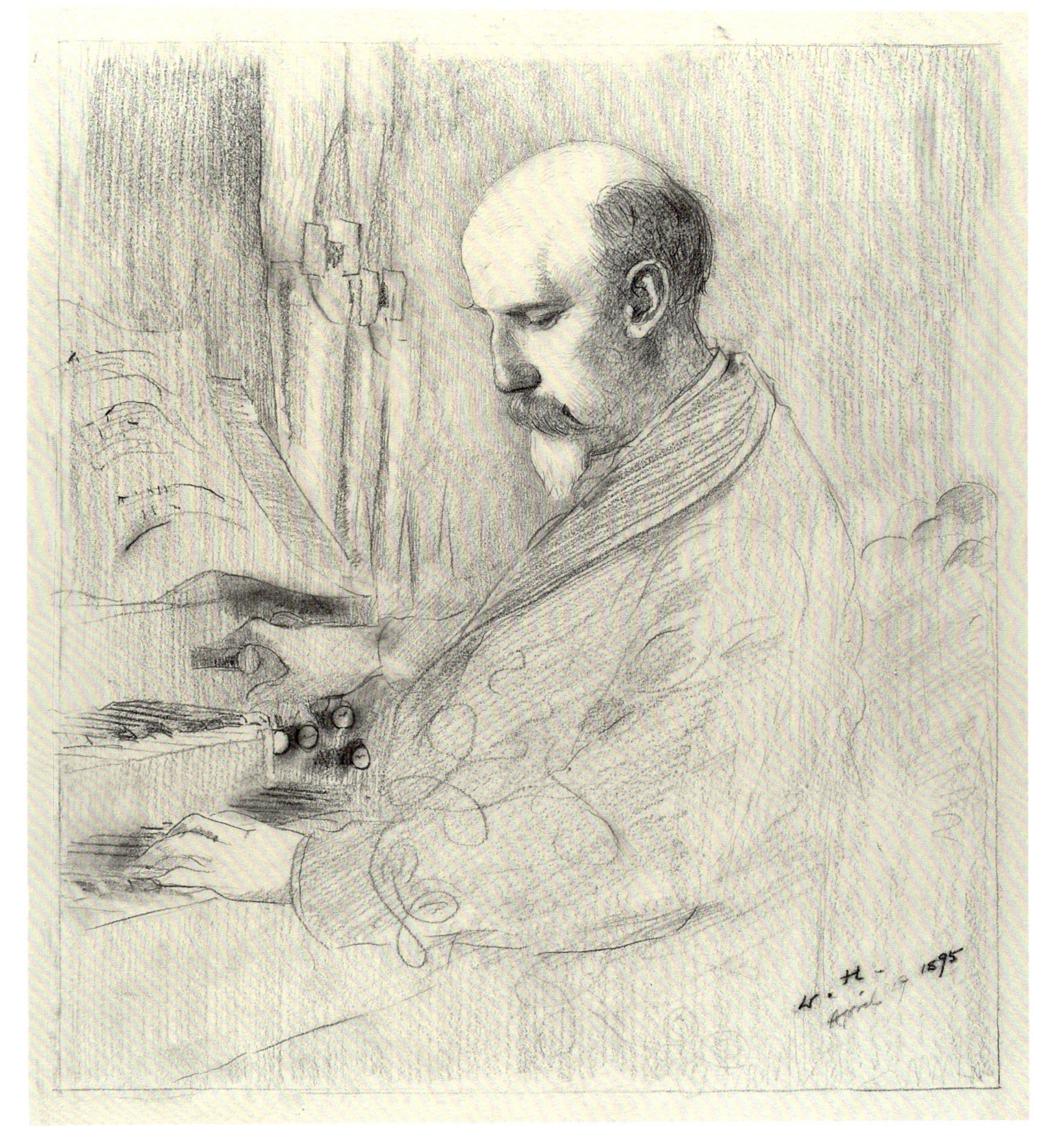


PORTRAIT OF BENJAMIN JOHNSON LANG N° 1991.19.3

# YOUNG DUCKS

**1897 WATERCOLOR ON WOVE PAPER**
**14 x 21 INCHES**

SIGNED LOWER LEFT: WINSLOW HOMER '97
BEQUEST OF CHARLES SHIPMAN PAYSON, 1988.55.13

Winslow Homer hunted and fished in the company of his older brother, Charles. The brothers frequented the North Woods Club in the Adirondacks and by 1893 were traveling to Quebec in search of sport. Ever perceptive to sartorial custom, Homer depicts the guide in the stern of the canoe in local French Canadian costume, complete with knit cap and red sash. Sixty-one years old when he painted *Young Ducks*, the artist no doubt envied the stamina of his companions, as well as their lives as natural men of the north as the nineteenth century waned.

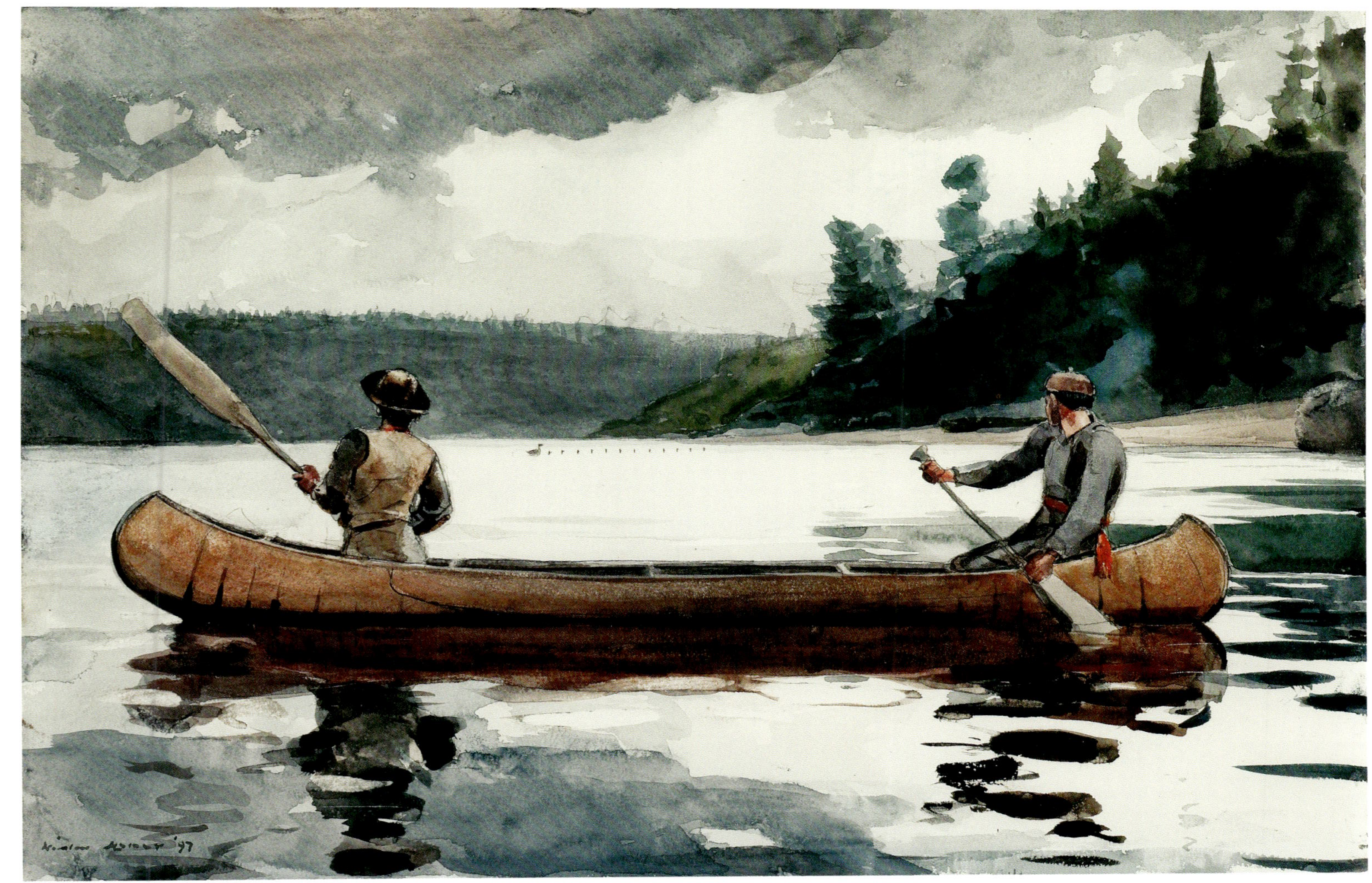

YOUNG DUCKS N° 1988.55.13

# WILD GEESE IN FLIGHT

**1897 OIL ON CANVAS**
**33 7/8 x 49 3/4 INCHES**

SIGNED LOWER RIGHT: HOMER 1897
BEQUEST OF CHARLES SHIPMAN PAYSON, 1988.55.2

The first owner of *Wild Geese in Flight* insisted later in life that the painting originally bore the title *At the Foot of the Lighthouse*. This shift in identification is telling, for it changes the image from a hunting scene with connotations of the sporting life and perhaps providing for human sustenance to a painting of caprice as the chance encounter with a lighthouse claims the geese without reason. The unseen navigational aid ironically becomes as fatal as bird shot from a hunter's blind.

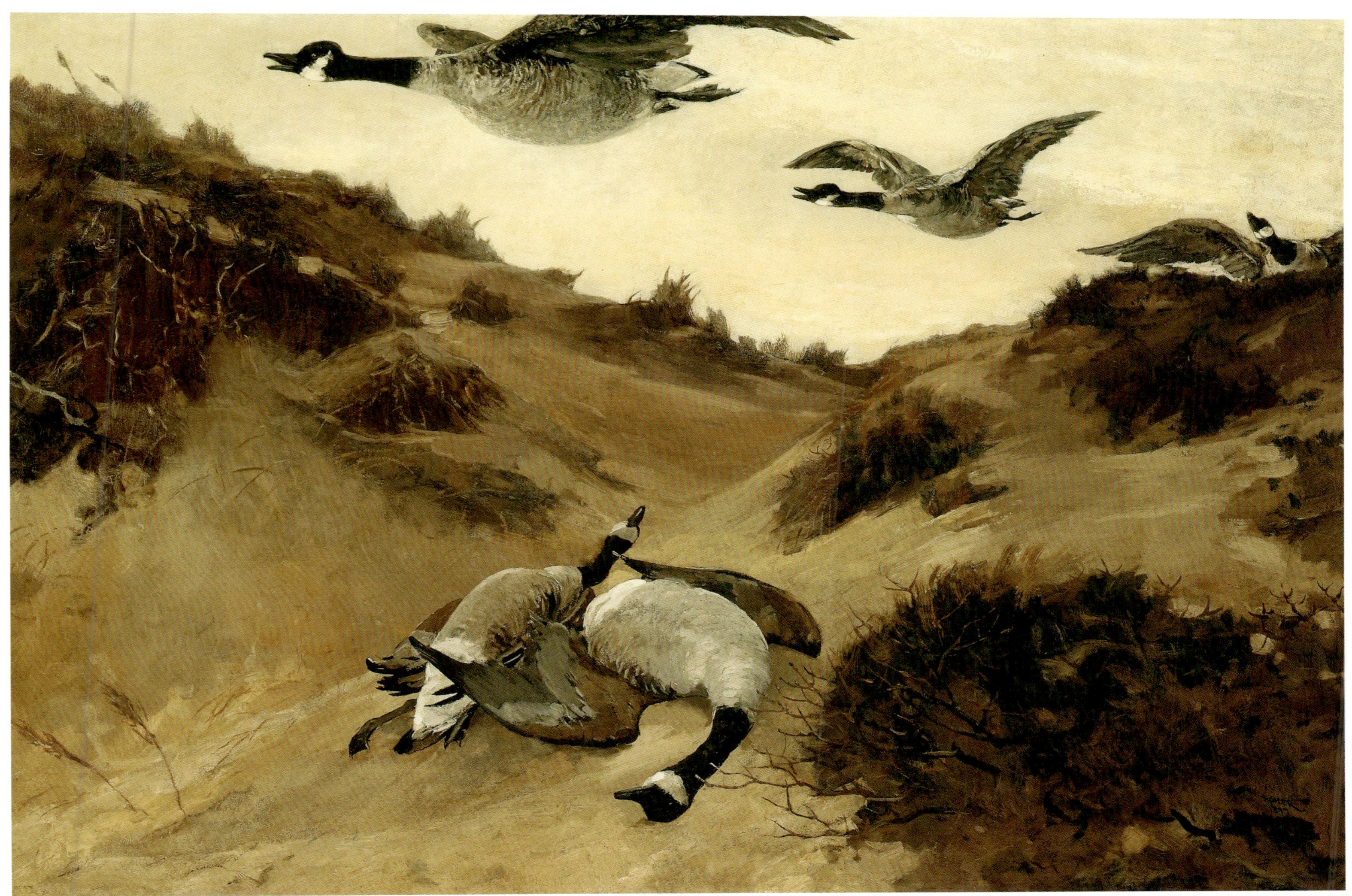

WILD GEESE IN FLIGHT N° 1988.55.2

Library of Congress Control Number: 2010924032

ISBN 978-0-916857-53-0

Photography Credits
Archives of American Art: fig. 5; Bowdoin College Museum of Art: figs. 1, 11–12;
Meyersphoto.com: figs. 2–4, 6–10, plates 1–20

This catalog was published in conjunction with the exhibition *Winslow Homer and the Poetics of Place*, June 5–September 6, 2010, which was organized by the Portland Museum of Art, Maine.

Presentation of this exhibition has been funded in part by a grant from the Maine Arts Commission, an independent state agency supported by the National Endowment for the Arts.

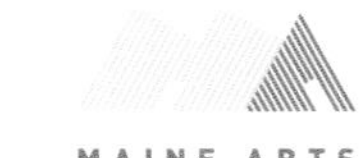


Designed by Daniel Pepice, Portland, Maine
Production by Sandra Klimt, Klimt Studio, Inc., Portland, Maine
Edited by Terry Reece Hackford, Newton, Massachusetts
Copyedited by Rickie Harvey, Boston, Massachusetts
Printed by Meridian Printing, East Greenwich, Rhode Island
Bound by Acme Bookbinding, Charlestown, Massachusetts

Cover image: Winslow Homer, *Weatherbeaten*, 1894, oil on canvas. Bequest of Charles Shipman Payson, 1988.55.1
Frontispiece: Winslow Homer, *Two Men in a Canoe*, 1895, watercolor on gray laid paper. Bequest of Charles Shipman Payson, 1988.55.12
Page 28: Winsor & Newton, *Winslow Homer's Watercolor Box*, circa 1900, canvas, leather, metal, watercolor, China white paint, wood, plastic. Museum purchase with support from Mr. and Mrs. L. Robert Porteous, Jr. in honor of Bennet C. Porteous, 1979.15.la-d